Melvil Dewey

Simplified Library School Rules

Card Catalog, Accession, Book Numbers, Shelf List, Capitals, Punctuation...

Melvil Dewey

Simplified Library School Rules
Card Catalog, Accession, Book Numbers, Shelf List, Capitals, Punctuation...

ISBN/EAN: 9783337159504

Printed in Europe, USA, Canada, Australia, Japan

Cover: Foto ©Lupo / pixelio.de

More available books at **www.hansebooks.com**

Simplified Library School Rules

CARD CATALOG   ACCESSION

BOOK NUMBERS   SHELF LIST

CAPITALS, PUNCTUATION, ABBREVIATIONS

LIBRARY HANDWRITING

BY

MELVIL DEWEY, M. A.

Director New York State Library and Library School

1898

Library Bureau

BOSTON   530 Atlantic Ave
NEW YORK: 377 Broadway   CHICAGO: 215 Madison St
PHILADELPHIA: 112-116 N. Broad St.   WASHINGTON, D. C   928 F St. N. W.
LONDON, W C : 10 Bloomsbury St.

CONTENTS

Preface	5
Definitions	6
Abbreviations	11
Simplified card catalog rules	
1 Checks	11
In books	11
a Main entry	11
b Cataloger	11
On cards	12
c Added entry	12
d Reference	12
e Added heading	12
f Accession number	12
2 Main entries, added entries and references	12
General	12
a Surname	12
b Initials	12
c Pseudonym	12
d Country, city, society, etc.	13
e Anonymous book	13
f Joint author	13
Special classes of books	13
g Commentary, translation	13
h Catalog	13
i College society and fraternity	14
j Serial	14
k Cyclopedia, directory, almanac	14
l Bible	14
m Sacred book, anonymous classic	14
Special classes of people	15
n Married women	15
o Noblemen	15
p Ecclesiastical dignitaries	15
q Persons enterd under forenames	15
Added entries and references	15
r Editor, translator, etc.	15
s Title	15
t Analytic	16
u Series	16
v References	16
w Other added entries and references	17
3 Form of heading	17
a Author entry	17
b Subject entry	17
c Added entry and reference	17
d Prefix	17
e Compound name	18
f Title of honor, date, etc.	18
g Government department	18
h Municipal department	18
i Society, institution	19
j Subordinate part of heading	19
k Inversion	19
4 Title	19
a Omissions	19
b Editor, translator	20
c Initial article	20
d Author's name	20
e Spelling	20
f Arabic figures	20
g Rare book	20
h Added edition	20
i Second copy	21
5 Imprint	21
a Arrangement	21
b Fulness	21
c Edition	21
d Incomplete work	21
e Continuation	22
f Size	22
g Atlas	22
h Map, broadside, etc.	22
i Place	22
j Date	22
k Analytic	22
6 Contents and notes	23
a Contents	23
b Notes	23
7 Subject entries	23
a Main entry	23
b Analytic	23
c Pamflets	23
8 Indention, spacing, call numbers	24
Indention	24
a Author	24
b Title	24
c Periodical, cyclopedia	24
d Subject heading	24
e Added entry for editor, translator, title, etc.	24
f Analytic	24
g Reference	24
h Note	24
i Contents and series	24
j Extra card	24
Spacing	25
k Heading	25

	l Title and imprint	25	
	Call numbers	25	
	m Position, etc.	25	
9	Arrangement	25	
	a Order	25	
	b Umlaut	25	
	c Person, place, title	25	
	d Surname	25	
	e Prefix	25	
	f Works	25	
	g Country, city, society, etc.	26	
	h Alfabeting	26	
10	Dictionary catalog	26	
	a Subject headings	26	
	b Sample cards	26	
	c Arrangement	26	
	d Record of subject headings	26	
11	Clast catalog	26	
	a Subject entry	26	
	b Added subject number	27	
	c Bible	27	
	d Biografy: clast catalog	27	
	e Biografy: name catalog	27	
	f Author bibliografy	27	
	g General criticism	27	
	h Criticism of an individual work	28	
	i Genealogy	28	
	j Local history	28	
	k Arrangement: clast catalog	28	
	l Arrangement: name catalog	28	
12	Colord cards	28	
	Sample cards	29	
Simplified accession rules			
20	Accession book	47	
	a Importance	47	
	b Form	47	
21	Reception	48	
	a Bill	48	
	b Order slip	48	
	c Book	48	
	d Private mark	48	
22	Entry	48	
	a Order	48	
	b Abbreviations, etc.	48	
	c Date of reception	48	
	d Accession number	49	
	e Number on book	49	
	f Number on card	49	
	g Pamflets	49	
	h Anthor	50	
	i Title	50	
	j Imprint	50	
	k Place and publisher	50	

l Year	50	
m Pages	50	
n Size	50	
o Binding	50	
p Source	51	
q Cost	51	
r Call number	51	
s Volume number	51	
t Second copy	51	
u Remarks	51	
v Pictures, statuary, maps, etc.	52	
23 Stamping, plating, pocketing, labeling	52	
a Stamping	52	
b Plating	52	
c Pocketing	52	
d Labeling	52	
Sample page from *Condensed accession book* ....facing	52	
Simplified book numbers		
30 Arrangement of books in each class	53	
31 Book numbers	53	
a Purpose	53	
b Principles	53	
c Form	54	
32 Arrangement by use of tables	54	
a Cutter tables	54	
b Author arrangement	54	
c Length of number	54	
d Extra figure	54	
e Large book	55	
33 Title marks	55	
a Arrangement of titles	55	
b Titles with same initial	55	
c Titles beginning with same two letters	55	
d Second copy	55	
34 Special classes	56	
a Juvenil books	56	
b Large classes	56	
c Local history and genealogy	56	
d Books about an author	56	
35 Individual biografy	56	
a General arrangement	56	
b Length of number	56	
c Several lives of same person	57	
d Authors having same initial	57	
36 Special schemes	57	
a Shakspere and other classics	57	
b Shakspere scheme	57	

Contents

c James Fenimore Cooper	58	
d Sir Walter Scott	59	
37 Arrangement without use of tables	59	
a Arbitrary title marks	59	

Simplified shelf list rules

40 Shelf list	61	
Importance	61	
Use	61	
a Inventory	61	
b Brief class catalog	61	
c Book numbers	61	
Form	61	
d Sheets	61	
e Cards	62	
41 Shelf list on sheets	62	
General	62	
a Arrangement of entries	62	
b Number of entries	62	
c Date	62	
d Class number	62	
e Book number	62	
f Accession number	62	
g Volume number	62	
h Author	62	
i Title	63	
j Unalfabeted entries	63	
k Old sheets	63	
Special cases	63	
l Second copy	63	
m Edition	63	
n Special location	63	
o Changed number	63	
Special classes	64	
p Serials	64	
q Individual biografy	64	
r Genealogy	64	
42 Shelf list on cards	65	
General	65	
a Size	65	
b Number of entries	65	
c Class and book number, author and title	65	
d Accession number	65	
Special cases	65	
e Second copy	65	
f Special location	65	
g Changed number	65	
Special classes	65	
h Serials	65	
i Individual biografy	65	
j Genealogy	65	
Sample cards	66	
Sample shelf sheets	66	

1 General	facing	66
2 Serials	facing	67

Capitals, punctuation, abbreviations

50 Capitals	68	
a First word	68	
b Book titles	68	
c Proper names	68	
d Proper adjectivs	68	
e I and O	68	
f Months, days, etc.	68	
g Epithets	69	
h Titles	69	
i Names of Deity	69	
j Abbreviations	69	
k Government departments, etc.	69	
l Events, etc.	69	
m Race	69	
51 Punctuation	69	
a Open punctuation	69	
b Title-pages	70	
c Redundancy	70	
d Omission of period	70	
e Use of period	70	
f Comma	70	
g Apostrofe	70	
h Dash	70	
i Curves	71	
52 Library abbreviations	71	
a Colon abbreviations	71	
b Other name abbreviations	71	
c Headings	72	
d Book titles	73	
e Imprint and notes	74	
f Size notation	74	
g Place of publication	75	
h States, titles, etc.	75	
i L. B. dates	77	
j Binding	77	

Library handwriting

60 Requirements	78	
a Legibility, speed	78	
b Uniformity	78	
61 Materials	78	
a Ink	78	
b Inkstands	78	
c Pens	78	
d Penholders	79	
e Erasers	79	
62 Alfabets	79	
Joind and disjoind hands	79	
63 Brief rules	79	
Joind hand	79	
a Position	79	

b Form...	79	i Figures ...	80
c Size ...	79	Disjoind hand...	80
d Slant ...	80	j Special letters...	80
e Spacing ...	80	Specimen alfabets and figures.	81
f Shading ...	80	Brief list of useful books on library economy...	83
g Uniformity ...	80		
h Special letters...	80	Index ...	85

PREFACE

These rules are based on *Library school rules*. The first edition of the catalog rules was issued in 1886 and was based on the *Condensed rules for an author and title catalog*, prepared by the cooperation committee of the A. L. A. and printed in the *Library journal*, 1883, 8:251-54, 263-64, and also separately. For an extended discussion of principles of cataloging, consult Cutter, *Rules for a dictionary catalogue, 3d edition*, 1891, cited in this book as Cutter, *Rules*. A compact summary of the principles of cataloging may be found in papers read at the Chicago meeting of the A. L. A., 1893, and publisht in *Papers prepared for the World's library congress*, p. 835-49.

The first part of the *Simplified card catalog rules* is devoted to rules which apply equally to a dictionary or a clast catalog. Where the rules for the two systems vary, the forms for the dictionary and the clast catalog are treated separately. Sample cards for both systems are also given, p. 29-46. As most popular libraries using a dictionary catalog have Cutter's *Rules for a dictionary catalogue* and the A. L. A. *List of subject headings for use in dictionary catalogs*, the rules and forms for subject headings are not repeated here.

The class numbers on the sample cards are assignd from the *Abridged decimal classification*. The book numbers are based on Cutter's *Alfabetic-order tables, altered and fitted with three figures by Kate E. Sanborn*.

For farther help in cataloging consult the *Catalog of 'A. L. A.' library*, 1893, where forms for both a dictionary and a clast catalog are illustrated. The *Catalog of 'A. L. A.' library* is also a valuable guide to the use of the *Expansive* as well as of the *Decimal classification*, as the carefully selected collection of 5000 volumes is classified by both systems. A brief list of books on library economy including these and others, and giving publisher and price, will be found on p. 83-84.

The labor of condensing and simplifying the *Library school rules* to adapt them better to the use of small libraries has fallen chiefly on the director's assistant, Miss Florence Woodworth, who has had the cooperation of Mr. W. S. Biscoe, Miss Mary L. Sutliff, and other members of the Library school faculty and of the New York state library staff, and to their painstaking and intelligent efforts the merits of the rules are largely due.

        MELVIL DEWEY
     Director New York State Library and Library School

DEFINITIONS

For the sake of clearness, the following technical terms occurring in the rules are defined.

Accession (*verb*)   To enter in an accession book.

Accession book.   The business record of volumes added to a library in order of receipt, giving a condenst description of the volume and the essential facts in its library history.—*Standard dictionary*

Accession number.   The number given to a volume in the order of its addition to a library.—*Standard dictionary*

Accession stamp.   A numbering stamp used in printing accession numbers in books, on cards, etc.

Added edition.   Another edition of a work already in the catalog.

Added entry.   A secondary entry; i. e. any other than a main entry.

Alfabetic subject catalog.   A catalog arranged alfabeticly by subject heads, usually without subdivisions.
  The term is also used to include alfabetico-clast catalogs.

Alfabetico-clast catalog.   An alfabetic subject catalog in which the subjects are groupt in broad classes with numerous alfabetic subdivisions. It may also include author and title entries in the same alfabet.

Analytic.   An added entry for a distinct part of a work or collection, which may be either a part or the whole of a volume or volumes, with or without a separate title-page. It may be either an author or a subject entry.

Analyze.   To make added entries for distinct parts of works.

Anonymous book.   A book in which the author's name is not on the title-page; but government or society publications are not anonymous if the author's name appears in any sub-title or half-title.
  Strictly no book is anonymous if the author's name appears anywhere in it.

Author card.   A card bearing an author entry; usually the main author card.

Author catalog.   An alfabetic catalog of author entries, and entries under editors, translators, etc. It also usually contains titles, but is then more properly calld an author and title catalog.   *See also* Name catalog.

Author entry.   An entry using as heading the name of the author, (whether personal or corporate) or some substitute for it. It may be either a main or an added entry.

Bibliografee.   One who is the subject of a bibliografy.

Definitions

Bibliografy. A list of the books of a particular author, printer, place or period, or on any particular theme; the literature of a subject *See also* Catalog.

Binder's title. The title letterd on the binding of a book.

Biografee. One who is the subject of a biografy.—MURRAY. *New English dictionary*

Book card. A card usually bearing the call number, author and title of the book to which it belongs, kept in the book when on the shelves, and filed at the loan desk when the book is lent.

Book number. One or more characters, used to distinguish an individual book from all others having the same class, shelf or other generic number.

Bookplate. A label, bearing a name, crest, monogram, or other design, pasted in or on a book to indicate its ownership, its position in a library, etc.—*Century dictionary*

Book pocket. A pocket, usually of manila paper, pasted inside a book cover to hold the book or borrower's card.

Bracket (*noun*) Rectangular inclosing marks [ ], as distinguisht from curves ( ).

——(*verb*) To inclose between brackets.—*Standard dictionary*

Broadside. A sheet of paper printed on one side only; e. g. posters, hand-bills, Thanksgiving proclamations, etc.

Call number. Characters indicating the location of a book on the shelves and distinguishing it from all others in the library. Usually composed of class and book number, or in fixt location, of shelf and book number.

Catalog. A list of books which is arranged on some definit plan. As distinguisht from a bibliografy, it is a list of books in some library or collection. For specific kinds of catalogs see:

Accession book	Dictionary catalog
Alfabetic subject catalog	Name catalog
Alfabetico-clast catalog	Shelf list
Author catalog	Subject catalog
Clast catalog	

Check. A conventional mark indicating that certain work is to be or has been done, or conveying other information.

Class number. One or more characters showing the class to which a book belongs. In a relativ location this also shows its place on the shelves.

Clast catalog. A catalog of subject entries arranged logically, usually by class numbers. If not arranged systematicly but by the alfabet, it is calld an alfabetic subject catalog. *See also* Alfabetic subject, Alfabetico-clast and Dictionary catalog.

Collate. To examin the sheets of a book by signatures or leaves, to ascertain whether they are perfect and in proper order.

Colon abbreviations. Abbreviations for the most common forenames of men and women; formd of the initial followd by : and .. for English names, by ; and ., for the German form, and by ! and ,. for the French. Originated by C: A. Cutter. See 52a.

Continuation. Any publication issued in parts at different times, whether serials, irregular publications or books.

Cross reference, *see* Reference.

Curves. The upright curves ( ) used to mark off an interjected explanatory clause or qualifying remark; marks of parenthesis.

Dictionary catalog. A catalog in which all entries (author, title, subject, etc.) are arranged in one alfabet like the words in a dictionary. It is distinguisht from other alfabetic catalogs: 1) by giving specific entry in all cases; and 2) by its individual entry.

Duplicate. A second copy of a book identical with the first in edition, contents and imprint, though binding and paper may differ.

Edition. The number of books, etc. of the same kind publisht together or without change of form or of contents. —*Century dictionary*

For a more exact use, see recommendations of the London publishers' association, *Publishers' weekly*, 19 Mar. 1898, 53:555.

Entry. The registry of a book in a catalog or list. *See also:*

    Added entry   Series entry
    Analytic   Subject entry
    Author entry   Title entry
    Main entry

Fixt location. System of marking and arranging books by shelf and book number so that their absolute position in room, tier and on shelf is always the same.

Fold symbol. A symbol indicating the number of leaves into which a sheet is folded, and thereby the approximate size of the page. See 52f.

Guide card. A projecting labeld card inserted in a card catalog to aid in finding a desired place or heading.

Half-binding. A binding in which the back, part of the sides and the corners are coverd with leather or some other binding material than paper.

Half-title. A shortend title at the head of the opening page of the text.

The short title-page preceding the full title-page is calld a bastard title.

Definitions

Heading. The word by which the alfabetic place of an entry in the catalog is determind, usually the name of the author, editor or translator, the name of the subject, or of the literary form (drama, poetry, etc.), or of the practical form (almanacs, dictionaries, etc.), or a word of the title.

Imprint. Bibliografic information concerning place, publisher and date; more broadly including also edition, size, pages, illustrations, etc.

Indention. The setting in of a line by a blank space at the beginning or left hand, as in the first line of a paragraf.—*Standard dictionary*

Individual entry. Entering a book under the name of a person or place as a subject heading; e. g. a life of Napoleon under Napoleon, not under Biografy; or a history of England under England, not under History.

Initials. A letter or letters used as a substitute for the author's name; e. g. H. H. for Helen Hunt.

L. B. dates. Library Bureau dates; a system of date abbreviations as brief as possible without ambiguity, devised and first used by the Library Bureau. See 52i.

Lower case letter. A small letter as distinguisht from a capital.

Main entry. The full or principal entry; usually the author entry. According to these rules it consists of author's name (3a) short title (4a) and imprint (5a).

Name catalog. A catalog including names of authors, editors, etc., also names of persons and places, used as subject headings. It also usually contains titles, like an author catalog.

Name reference. A reference from alternativ forms of name to that selected for use in the catalog.

Order index. Alfabetic file of outstanding order slips.

Order slip. Printed slip with spaces for recording author, title, imprint and other items needed in ordering books for a library.

Pseudonym. A fictitious name assumed by an author to conceal his identity.—*Century dictionary*

Receipt index. Alfabetic file of order slips for books receivd.

Recto. The right-hand page of an open book; the opposit of verso. Rectos bear odd, versos even numbers.

Reference. A direction referring from one heading to another. *See also* Name reference; Subject reference.

Relativ location. An arrangement of books according to their relations to each other and regardless of the shelves or rooms where they are then placed. Relativ location admits indefinit intercalation and moving to other shelves or rooms without altering the call numbers. Alfabetic arrangement is one form of relativ location.

Running title. A title or headline repeated at the head of succeeding pages, as throughout a book or chapter.—*Standard dictionary*

Secondary entry, *see* Added entry.

Serial. A publication issued in successiv parts, usually at regular intervals, and continued indefinitly.

Series entry. An entry using as heading the name of a series, or its editor and title, followd by a list of the books in the library belonging to the series.

Series note. Name of series to which a book belongs, either editor and title or title alone; according to these rules, written in curves ( ) after the imprint.

Shelf list. A brief inventory of the books in a library, the entries arranged in the order of the books on the shelves. It is generally for official use only.

Shelf number. In fixt location a number indicating the location of a special shelf; also used as a synonym for call or location number.

Signature. A distinguishing mark, letter or number placed usually at the bottom of the first page of each form or sheet of a book to indicate its order to the folder and binder. Hence, the form or sheet on which such a mark is placed, considerd as a fractional part of a book; as, 'the work is printed in 20 signatures'.—*Standard dictionary*

Size letters. A series of abbreviations, chiefly single letters, to indicate the sizes of books. See 52f.
Adopted for the use of the A. L. A. in 1878; see *Library journal*, 1878, 3:19.

Size mark. One or more characters to designate the size of a book. The most common are the fold symbol and the size letter. See 52f.

Size rule. A metric rule on which are stampt the size letters and the corresponding fold symbols.

Standard sizes. A series of fixt sizes for cards, blanks and other library fittings and supplies adopted, after extended experiments, as best fitted to promote uniformity and cooperation among libraries. For list and discussion see *Library notes*, v. 2, no 5: 46-53.

Subject card. A card bearing a subject entry.

Subject catalog. A catalog of subjects, arranged by class numbers or alfabeted by names of subjects

Subject entry. An entry with class numbers or subject headings or combination of the two to determin its place in a subject catalog. It may be either a main or an added entry.

Subject heading. A name of a subject used as a heading under which books relating to that subject are enterd.

Subject reference. A reference from one subject, name or number to another, either a synonym, an allied heading, a more minute division of the subject or a more general subject.

Title. The distinguishing name of any written production. It usually refers to all the matter on the title-page except the author's name and the imprint. *See also* Binder's title; Half title.

Title entry. An entry using as a heading the title or some part of it.

Title mark. That part of the book number which is used to distinguish different books by the same author; e. g. the book number for Shakspere's, *Macbeth* is S5ma of which the first part, S5, stands for Shakspere and the second part, ma, is the title mark for *Macbeth*.

Verso. The left-hand page of an open book; the opposit of recto.

ABBREVIATIONS
For library abbreviations, see 52, p. 71-77

A. L. A.	American library association
cm	Centimeter, the $\frac{1}{100}$ of a meter; equal to 0.3937 + of an English inch, that is one inch equals 2.54 cm.
L. A. U. K.	Library association of the United Kingdom
L. B.	Library Bureau
P size	Postcard size, 7.5 x 12.5 cm (3 x 5 in. approximately)
S. C.	Sample card; referring to facsimile cards illustrating *Simplified card catalog rules*, p. 29-46

SIMPLIFIED CARD CATALOG RULES

1 Checks

When checks are used as a record of work done, they must not be put on till the work is actually finisht.

In books

1a **Main entry.** Pencil lightly on the title-page three dots […] under first letter of heading under which main entry is made. S. C. 58.

This check may be used either as a guide to catalogers or as a record of main entry.

In all cases when the heading selected for the main author entry does not appear on the title-page it should be inserted neatly on the title-page with a hard pencil.

1b **Cataloger.** To show by whom a book is catalogd, the cataloger's initials may be written on inner margin of first recto after title-page; e. g. C. F.

On cards

1c Added entry. On main card, place two dots [..] under first letter of headings for editor, translator, title, series, etc. S. C. 1, 5, 17, 27, 30, 32, 39, 42.

1d Reference. On main card, use a cross [x] to indicate references from other forms of names, pseudonyms, initials, etc. (S. C. 22, 25, 47) also on series card for editor or title of series. S. C. 36.

1e Added heading. If word to be checkt does not occur on face of card, either in heading, title, or note, write it on the back.

Always write entries on the back of the card so that they can be read from the front of the drawer by simply tipping the card forward. For recording entries for pamflet volumes, see 7c; for subject analytics, 2t; for subject headings in a dictionary catalog, 10d. S. C. 67.

1f Accession number. On back of main author card write accession number of the book. S. C. 67.

For accession number of second copy of a book, see 4i; for pamflet volumes, 7c. See also *Simplified accession rules*, 22f.

In case of long sets when the accession numbers are not consecutiv, after the first accession number write 'See shelf list.'

2 Main entries, added entries and references
General

2a Surname. Enter under surname of person who is responsible for the work, if this is known. He may be author (S. C. 1, 5, etc.), translator, editor (S. C. 20), compiler, etc.

If a work is enterd under name of editor, translator, compiler, etc., add ed., tr., comp., etc. 1 cm after the name. S. C. 20.

If a work is enterd under compiler, etc., usually give enough of title to show that the book is a collection; e. g. Hunt, Leigh, comp. *Book for a corner; or, Selections in prose and verse.*

2b Initials. Enter under author's initials when only these are known, putting last initial first; e. g. W, M. *Easter bells.* S. C. 21. Make also added entry under title. When author's name is found, fill it in on all cards and write a new card referring from initials to full name. S. C. 22-23.

If the book is likely to be lookt for under first initial, make also a reference from that; e. g. A. L. O. E. see Tucker, Charlotte Maria S. C. 24.

2c Pseudonym. Enter under pseudonym when real name can not be found; e. g. Junius, pseud. Also enter under pseudonym with reference from real name when the author is decidedly better known by his pseudonym. S. C. 27, 28.

Add the abbreviation 'pseud.' on all cards, 1 cm after the pseudonym used as heading; e. g. Eliot, George, pseud.

When, according to general rule 2a, the book is enterd under real name, make reference from pseudonym. S. C. 26.

Make added title entries for all pseudonymous books.

Both the real name and pseudonym may be given on a guide card. See 3f.

Simplified Card Catalog Rules 13

2d Country, city, society, etc. Enter under a country, city, society, institution or other body responsible for publication of the work. S. C. 51, 53 54. See also 3g–i.

After names of all except very prominent cities add country or state in ( ), e. g. Boston (Eng), Utica (N. Y) Also, if necessary to distinguish, add (state), (city), or (country); e. g. N. Y. (state). S. C. 16, 55. For alfabetic arrrangement see 9g.

2e Anonymous book. Enter under first word of title of an anonymous book whose author is still unknown, beginning on second line of card. S. C. 15–16, 72. When author's name is found, pencil it on title-page and enter on top line of card, making also a new card with added entry under title, followd by author's name. S. C. 17 19.

For entry of a periodical see 2j. For entry of a cyclopedia, directory or almanac, see 2k.

In entering under first word, disregard articles, serial numbers, mottoes and designations of series. See 4c.

When author's name is not in title of first volume, but is in that of any other, catalog like an anonymous book.

2f Joint author. Enter a book having more than one author under the first named in title. If only two authors, include both names in main heading; e. g. Lamb, Charles & Lamb, Mary, and make an added entry under the second. S. C. 30–31. If more than two, enter under the first '& others'; e. g. Roe, Richard & others (S. C. 57) making an added entry under each of the others only when of special importance.

If an author has more than one forename write the full name only once, and that on his own author card. S. C. 30–31.

When a work has joint editors, commentators or translators, if added entries are made for them (2r), they should be made separately (S. C. 6) not like joint authors.

Parties in a debate are treated like joint authors.

Distinguish between joint authors; e. g. Carlyle and Emerson, *Correspondence* and authors of separate works publisht together; e. g. Goldsmith and Johnson, *Vicar of Wakefield* and *Rasselas*. S. C. 42–43.

Special classes of books

2g Commentary, translation. Enter a commentary accompanied by text, or a translation, under same heading as original work, with added entry under commentator or translator when the work is commonly known by his name. For joint commentators see 2f.

Enter a commentary without text under commentator only, tho clast with the original; e. g. enter Coleridge, *Notes and lectures on Shakspeare* under Coleridge.

For entries in a dictionary catalog see Cutter, *Rules*, § 12.

2h Catalog. Enter the catalog of a private collection under owner; e. g. Choate, Rufus, *Catalogue of his library*.

Enter the catalog of a public collection under the body responsible for its publication (2d); e. g. Boston athenaeum, *Catalogue of the library*. S. C. 54.

2i College society and fraternity. Enter alumni proceedings, etc. and local college societies under college; e. g. Yale university—Skull and Bones society, with reference from Skull and Bones society.

Enter chapters of fraternities under name of fraternity, with reference from college; e. g. Phi Beta Kappa fraternity, Yale university, with reference from Yale university.

2j Serial. Enter a periodical under first word of title, beginning on first line of card. S. C. 47. For imprint see 5c.

In case of change of name of periodicals, make references from other name or names; e. g. *Christian union*, see *Outlook*. S. C 47-48.

In cataloging a periodical which has changed its name, prefer latest form. A set once catalogd under an earlier name should usually not be changed from that form to a later, as the gain is hardly worth the extra work involvd in recataloging.

Enter a periodical which is the organ of a society or club, under name of periodical, with added entry under name of society if needed; e. g. *Library journal ; official organ of the American library association*, under title.

Enter regular proceedings or transactions of a society, etc. under society's name with added entry under title, if needed; e. g. *Quarterly journal of the Geological society of London*, under society's name with added entry under title.

2k Cyclopedia, directory, almanac. Enter a general cyclopedia, city directory or almanac, under title, like a periodical, 2j, S. C. 49, making added entry for editor, publisher, partial title, or any form under which it may be known; e. g. enter *American cyclopaedia* under its title with added entry for Appleton, pub. But enter the work of an individual under author's name with added entry under title; e. g. Larousse, Pierre, *Grand dictionnaire universel du 19e siècle;* Chambers, William & Chambers, Robert, *Information for the people; a popular cyclopaedia*.

2l Bible. For treatment of *Bible* in a dictionary catalog, see Cutter. *Rules*, § 68. See also A. L. A. *List of subject headings*, 1898, p. 203-4. S. C. 62.

For treatment when clast and name catalogs are made, see 11c. S. C. 72-73.

2m Sacred book, anonymous classic. Enter *Talmud, Koran, Vedas* and other sacred books under their names as given in list below, beginning these headings on top line of card. Make added entries under editors, translators, etc. if the book is well known by their names.

Similarly, enter an anonymous classic of any literature under its best known title; e. g. *Beowulf, Nibelungenlied, Roland, Arabian nights' entertainments*. S. C. 13, 56.

The following is a list of the most common of these headings:

Anglo-Saxon chronicle	Domesday book
Arabian nights' entertainments	Federalist
Avesta	Fridthjófs saga frackna
Beowulf	Gesta Romanorum
Cid, Poem of the	Gudrun

Heliand
Hitopadesa
Kabala
Kalevala
Koran
Mabinogion
Mahábhárata
Merlin
Nibelungenlied
Renard the fox
Roland
Talmud
Upanishads

Special classes of people

2n Married women. Enter married women, and other persons who have changed their names, under the last well-known form, with reference, if necessary, from other forms; e. g. Helen Hunt under Jackson, Mrs Helen Hunt, with references from Hunt, and H. H ; Margaret Fuller under Fuller, with reference from Ossoli, Margaret Fuller, marchesa d'.

2o Noblemen. Enter a nobleman under his highest title with reference from family name; e. g. Romney, Henry Sidney, earl of. S. C. 7. If family name, or a lower title, is decidedly better known, enter under that with reference from title; e. g. Bacon, Francis, viscount St Albans, making reference from St Albans.

2p Ecclesiastical dignitaries. Enter an ecclesiastical dignitary, unless a pope or sovereign, under his surname; e. g. Newman, John Henry, card.; Butler, Joseph, bp. Make reference from title when surname does not appear on title-page; e. g. enter under Sherlock, Thomas, bp, and since Sherlock does not appear on title-page, make reference from Salisbury, Thomas, bp. of.

2q Persons entered under forenames. Enter a person known generally by a forename under that name; e. g.

sovereign	Napoleon 1, S. C. 33
ruling prince	Maximilian 1, elector of Bavaria
many oriental writers	Omar Khayyám
pope	Leo 13
friar	Hyacinthe, Père, Charles Loyson
person canonized	Augustine, St

Refer, if necessary, from other forms, e. g Bonaparte Napoleon, see Napoleon 1; Khayyám, Omar, see Omar Khayyám; Loyson, Charles, see Hyacinthe, Père, Charles Loyson.

Use arabic figures after the names of rulers, popes, etc.

Added entries and references

2r Editor, translator, etc. Make added entries for editors, translators, etc. only when book is well-known under those names; e. g. Longfellow's translation of the *Divine comedy*, Bryant's translation of the *Iliad*. Add ed., tr., etc. 1 cm after the name. S. C. 6.

2s Title. Make added entries under titles of all anonymous and pseudonymous books, or books enterd under initials, all novels, single poems and plays publisht separately, and all other striking titles; also under specially noticeable words in titles, unless these are provided for, in a dictionary catalog, by subject entries. S. C. 2, 18, 29, 41. If a book is well known by any title (e. g. running, half, or binder's title) differing from title-page make added entry under this other title.

In case of such works as the Iliad, Shakspere's plays, etc. where the library has many editions, a title reference instead of a title entry may be made; e. g. Iliad, see Homer. S. C. 14.

In fiction where there are several copies of the same book (see 4h-i) a single title card may be made for all, omitting date.

2t **Analytic.** Make analytics for distinct, important parts of books, specially when the parts have been publisht separately or when the subjects are not otherwise represented in the library. For form of imprint, see 5k. S. C. 39-46, 66, 71.

These analytics may be for an author (S. C. 40, 43), subject (S. C. 44-46, 66, 71), or title (S. C. 41.) Author analytics should not be made for parts of an author's collected works.

The writer of part of a book who also edits the whole work, has no author analytic, if editor card is made (2r) unless the part has been publisht separately.

On the back of every author analytic which has a corresponding subject card write its subject heading, or in a clast catalog, its subject number.

This often saves reference to main card, when for example, all the cards for an author must be removed from the catalog for correction, etc.

2u **Series.** Enter series usually under title (S. C. 34); or under editor if the series is better known by his name (S. C. 36).

In the former case make reference from editor only when series is also well known by his name; e. g. enter *English men of letters; ed. by John Morley*, under title with reference from Morley. S. C. 35.

If series is enterd under editor, always make reference from title; e. g. enter Arber, Edward, *English reprints*, under Arber, with reference from *English reprints*. S. C. 36-37.

Make series card only for more important series, but in all cases make series note in curves ( ) following date on main card. Give series number if important. S. C. 32-33, 38.

Give two lines to each item of contents on series card beginning with series number between red lines, thus allowing space for both class and book numbers. S. C. 34, 36.

For fulness of author's name on series card, follow rule for subject headings, 3b.

When extra cards are used give author and title briefly on back of card, to identify if misplaced. For indention of extra card, see 8j, S. C. 34, 47.

2v **References.** Make references to the form chosen for the heading, from any other form under which the reader is likely to look; e. g.

cities	3i	S. C. 55
college societies	2i	
compound names	3e	S. C. 8
ecclesiastical dignitaries	2p	
editors and titles of series	2u	S. C. 35, 37
forenames	2q	
government departments to bureaus	3g	S. C. 52
initials	2b	S. C. 23-24
married women	2n	
noblemen	2o	S. C. 7

periodicals	2j	S. C. 48
prefixes	3d	S. C. 11, 12
pseudonyms	2c	S. C. 26
spellings	3a	S. C. 13
title	2s	S. C. 14
umlaut	9b	S. C. 9, 10

For form of author's name and indention, see 3c, 8g.
For references from *Bible*, single books of the *Bible*, etc. when a class catalog is made, see 11c S. C. 73.

2w Other added entries and references. Make added entries or references whenever needed for ready finding of a book.

3 Form of heading

3a Author entry. On author card use best known form of author's name, with reference from any other form commonly known.

The *Catalog of 'A. L. A.' library* will serve as a guide. This rule will sometimes override the more specific rules which follow. They usually determin the heading unless some other form is clearly better known. For treatment of pseudonyms, see 2c.

For form of names for Greek and Latin authors follow Smith, *Dictionary of Greek and Roman biography.*

In headings and notes if there is good authority for more than one spelling, prefer the shorter; e. g. Shakspere, not Shakespeare.

Give author's hereditary titles in the language in which the name is enterd: e. g. Paris, Louis Philippe, comte de. For sovereigns, reigning princes and popes, always use English form of title.

3b Subject entry. On subject cards write out author's forename if only one; e. g. Phillips, Wendell. If more than one forename is used on author card, e. g. Beecher, Henry Ward, give simply initials or colon abbreviations on subject card; e. g. Beecher, H: W. S. C. 3-4, 33.

Write all surnames in full on subject card: e. g. Beaconsfield, Benjamin Disraeli, earl of; Jackson, Mrs Helen Hunt.

Use colon abbreviations for English names, where only initials would otherwise be given, H: meaning Henry and being as brief as H. S. C. 3-4, 33.

3c Added entry and reference. On added entry cards for editor, translator, etc. write editor's or translator's name on top line in the form for heading on author cards. See 3a. S C. 6. Write author's name on second line in the form for heading on subject cards. See 3b. S. C. 2, 6. For indention, see 8e.

On name reference cards write author's name on second line in form for heading on author cards. See 3a. S. C. 7-10, 12, 13, 26, 28. For indention, see 8g.

3d Prefix. Enter English and French surnames beginning with a prefix (except the French de and d') under prefix; in other languages under word following (S. C. 10-12) e. g. La Fontaine, Jean de;

Voltaire, François Marie Arouet de; Goethe, Johann Wolfgang von, Lennep, Jacob van, but enter foreign names anglicized under prefix, e. g. De Quincey, Van Nostrand. Make references whenever the name would be lookt for under a form not chosen; e. g. De Staël, Mme, see Staül, Mme de.

Most French names, however, would be lookt for under part following de, making reference unnecessary; e. g. Sévigné, Mme de.

3e Compound name. Enter English compound names under last part, foreign under first, with reference from form not chosen; e. g. enter Sabine Baring-Gould, under Gould, Sabine Baring-, with reference from Baring-Gould, and Eugen von Böhm-Bawerk under Böhm-Bawerk, with reference from Bawerk, Eugen von Böhm-. S. C. 8.

According to 3a, James Orchard Halliwell-Phillipps is better enterd under Halliwell Phillipps.

3f Title of honor, date, etc. Add titles of honor, dates of birth and death, residence, etc. to *distinguish* writers of same name.

Always add titles that are part of the person's usual designation, as Rev., Gen. etc. or a sobriquet; e. g. Jackson, Gen. Thomas Jonathan, called Stonewall. Distinguishing dates follow title affixes, and precede affixes ed. tr. etc.; e. g. Brown, John, D.D. 1715-66, tr.

Dates of birth and death and other information in regard to author may be given on a guide card; e. g. Howard, Blanche Willis, afterwards Mrs Teuffel. See *Catalog of 'A. L. A. library,'* under Howard, p. 406; see also under Holland, Josiah Gilbert, p. 403, and under Sand, George, p. 514.

3g Government department. Enter government departments (country or state) including national or royal libraries, museums, galleries, etc. under name of country, etc. followd by a dash and official name of department, inverting if necessary to alfabet by the distinctiv word (3j-k, 9g): e. g. U. S.—Agriculture, Dep't of; Gr. Br.—National gallery, London, with reference from National gallery, London, and London National gallery.) Do not invert.

Enter subordinate bureaus directly under name of bureau, and under department give a list of all bureaus belonging to it under which entries have been made; e. g. U. S.—Education, Bureau of, and make reference from U. S.—Interior, Dep't of. S. C. 51-52.

Always give name of country in English form; e. g. Austria not Österreich.

3h Municipal department. Enter departments of cities, towns, etc. under name of place followd by dash and official name of department (3j-k, 9g), as in government departments (3g); e. g.

    Boston—Public library.
    Cincinnati—Education, Board of.
    Minneapolis—Health, Board of.

This includes libraries, galleries, etc. controld by city governments but not others.

Always give name of cities, towns, etc. in English form: e. g. Vienna not Wien, Florence not Firenze

Simplified Card Catalog Rules

3i Society, institution. Enter a society or other institution under its best known name; in case of doubt, under first word, not an article, of its corporate name. Make reference from any other well known name, specially from name of place in which it has headquarters (S. C. 54–55); e. g.

    Royal society of London, with reference from London, Royal society of.

    Corcoran gallery of art, Washington, with reference from Washington (D. C.), Corcoran gallery of art.

    Enoch Pratt free library of Baltimore, with reference from Baltimore, Enoch Pratt free library of

    Lawrence scientific school, with reference from Harvard university—Lawrence scientific school.

    University of Chicago, with reference from Chicago University.

    New York Shakespeare society, with reference from Shakespeare society of New York.

    Elizabeth (N. J.), First presbyterian church, with reference from First presbyterian church, Elizabeth (N. J.)

    New Jersey medical society, with reference from Medical society of New Jersey.

    Pennsylvania historical society, with reference from Historical society of Pennsylvania.

Spell the names of societies, etc. as in their publications; e. g. New York Shakespeare society, with reference, if necessary, from other forms.

For arrangement, see 9g.

3j Subordinate part of heading. Use a dash [—] in headings between name of a country, city, town or institution and name of a department, bureau or other subordinate part; e. g. Boston—Public library.

This is done for convenience in arrangement, thus separating names of official bodies from names of institutions, etc. beginning with name of place e g Brooklyn—Public instruction, Sup't of; Brooklyn civil service reform association. See 9g. S. C. 51–52.

3k Inversion. Use inversion to bring most important word of a heading first: e. g. Scribner's, Charles, sons; Cincinnati—Education, Board of. S. C. 51–52, 55. See also 9g.

4 Title

4a Omissions. Give short title, omitting:

    mottoes
    repetitions
    author's name
    editors, translators, etc. unless important
    all honorary titles
    usually initial article in English and all other non-essential matter. S. C. 58, 1, 5, 15, 22, 25, 30, 38–39, 44, 50–51, 56–57, 63–66, 68–72, 74, etc.

Put serial number, designation of series and imprint information into imprint or series note on main card.

Disregard engraved and illustrated title-pages except when there is no other title-page.

On main and added entry subject cards give enough of title to justify the subject entry, or if title does not show it, give information in a note.

4b Editor, translator. When editors, translators, etc. are given in title, follow rule for author's name on subject card. See 3b. S. C. 5, 56-58.

4c Initial article. Use initial article in English when needed to complete the sense; e. g. (*The*) *judgment*, (*A*) *vision*. In other languages always express the article. Inclose initial article in curves ( ) and alfabet by following word. S. C. 62.

4d Author's name. Repeat author's name in title in those few cases in which it is an integral part of title; e. g. *Monteith's geography*.

4e Spelling. Follow title-page in spelling and in use of umlaut, writing e. g. Shakspere or Shakespeare, Goethe or Göthe, as words appear on title-page.

Indicate misprints, or odd spellings, by three dots underneath, rather than by the common [*sic*]; e. g. Kanzas not Kanzas [*sic*]. S. C. 36, 38, 44-45.

4f Arabic figures. In book titles use arabic figures for all numbers above nine. Numbers below 10 may be written out unless figures are used on title-page. Numbers at beginning of a title or in any other specially prominent place may be written out. The clumsy and easily misread roman numerals should always be given in arabic. S. C. 15, 49, 56, 63.

Figures may be used for all numeral adjectivs; e. g. 2d, 4th.

4g Rare book. Titles of books specially valuable for antiquity or rarity may be given in full, with all practicable precision, or reference may be made to bibliografies in which they are fully described. See Cutter, *Rules*, §261.

4h Added edition. In adding another entry to a card, use a single dash [—] in place of author heading, and two dashes [— —] in place of author and title. S. C. 17-19, 49.

Usually add later to earlier editions in this way, giving imprint of second entry and part of title if it differs in important particulars.

Indexes, supplements, keys, etc., are added to card with one or two dashes, inverting, if necessary, to bring words 'index,' etc. first. S. C. 49.

On back of main card write accession number or numbers of edition added, using imprint date or number of edition to distinguish them; e. g.

    2763-4 2v. 1870
    8749-50 2v. 1896

In fiction ignore difference of editions and translations, treating them as 'copies' (4i) unless there are more than minor changes; e. g. a differ-

Simplified Card Catalog Rules

ent number of volumes, or unless one edition is sufficiently well known to be called for in preference to others.

4i Second copy. In case of a second copy of a book, on main and added entry cards write '2 cop.' in red ink at right of book or class number, diagonally (/) in blank space between red lines. S. C. 63-66.

In case of fiction and other popular books where number of copies is continually changing, number of copies may be omitted from face of card.

On back of main card write after old accession number 'cop. 1'; after new accession number, 'cop. 2'; e. g. 943   cop. 1
8706   cop. 2 S. C. 67.

If two copies come in at same time write accession number on back of card as if for two volumes, but instead of '2 v.' write '2 cop.'; e. g. 4675 6 2 cop.

5 Imprint

5a Arrangement. Arrange the imprint in three groups 1 cm apart as follows, (S. C. 1, 47, 49-51, 53, 56-57, 72, etc.)

1	edition	See 5c. S. C. 49, 51, 58.
2	volumes	If more than one. S. C. 49. See also 5d-e.
	illus.	When book is really illustrated. S. C. 49.
	maps	Always specify maps. S. C. 20, 49. See also 5h.
	size	By size letter, see 52f. S. C. 1, 15, 20, etc. See also 5f-h.
3	place	First place of publication. S. C. 49. See also 5i. S. C. 21.
	date	See 5j. S. C. 1, 20, 21, 49.

5b Fulness. Write full imprint only on main cards. S. C. 1, 3, 15-17, 19, 32-33, 38, 63-64, 68-69.

For added entries, the number of volumes, if more than one, and date are sufficient. S. C. 2, 6, 29, 31. See also 2s.

5c Edition. Give edition in English when it forms a group of the imprint; and begin with a capital. Omit all adjectivs except new, revized, enlarged, and number of edition, translating equivalent phrases into these; e. g. Ed. 2 enl. not 2te durchgesehene, vermehrte & verbesserte auflage. S. C. 17, 30, 49, 51, 58.

Give edition in language of title-page if it is copied as a part of title.

When volumes of a set are of different editions, give earliest and latest editions; e. g. Ed. 1-4.

When designation of edition is in nature of a series, give it in a series note, e. g. Household ed.; Riverside ed. See 2u. S. C. 42.

5d Incomplete work. When volumes of a set are missing, give number of volumes in complete set, specifying missing volumes in pencil note, which can be erased as soon as they are secured. S. C. 53. For continuations, see 5e.

If a book is incomplete and no more will be publisht, give in the imprint in ink what has appeard, adding in a note 'No more publisht.' S. C. 53.

5e Continuation. In continuations omit volumes from imprint, and give below in columns exact statement of volumes in library with dates which they cover. S. C. 47. Add new volumes in order as receivd; e. g.
Smithsonian institution — Regents, Board of.
    Annual report.   illus. O.   Wash. 1847 — *date*.
    Library has:
v. 1-10   1846-55

    12-49   1857-94
    50   1894-95
    51   1895-96

On subject card, if any, in a dictionary catalog, add note; e. g. 'For full statement of volumes in library see *Harper's monthly* in main alfabet.'

In a clast catalog add note to main subject card, 'For full statement of volumes in library, see name catalog.'

5f Size. If volumes of a set have different sizes give both sizes; e. g. 12 v. O & Q; or, if set is incomplete, v. 1-8, O & Q. If the size makes a different call number necessary, give at left the call number for such volumes, followd by number and size of volumes; e. g.
$\frac{942}{\text{qI}^{r}73}$ v. 5-12, Q. S. C. 50. See also *Simplified book numbers*, 32e.

5g Atlas. If there is an atlas or volumes of plates, write; e. g. v. 1-12, O & atlas F, or if they are of same size, v. 1-12 & atlas O. S. C. 50.

5h Map, broadside, etc. If maps, broadsides, etc. are catalogd separately, give size of map in centimeters, hight by width; e. g. 91x71 cm. S. C. 57.

5i Place. Give place in language in which it appears on title-page. Give corrections and additions in English; e. g. Camb. Eng., Camb. Mass.

When different volumes of a long set are publisht in many different places, write 'Various places' in imprint.

If place of publication is not known, write n. p. meaning 'no place' in imprint. S. C. 21.

5j Date. When volumes of a set have different dates, give earliest and latest dates; e. g. 1834-49. S. C. 49.

If practicable, supply date if it does not appear on title-page; e. g. use copyright date, preface date, etc   S. C. 20, 47.

Use approximate dates if these only are known; e. g. ? 1893, 189—, 18—. As a last resort use n. d. meaning no date.' S. C. 21.

5k Analytic. In analytics, give author and title of part analyzed, followd by a brief reference to complete work in curves ( ). S. C. 40-41, 43-46, 66, 71.

When the article has an independent title-page give imprint of analyzed part before the ( ). S. C. 44-45.

If it is a part of the regular pages or is contained in preface or appendix pages, give page where analytic begins. S. C. 40-41, 43, 46.

6 Contents and notes

6a Contents. Give contents of volumes, when necessary properly to describe the work.

It is usually best to give contents only on one card. In literature and polygrafy they are more useful on author card, in other classes, generally on subject cant.

Contents should be written in smaller letters. Begin on second line after imprint; see also 8i. S. C. 5.

6b Notes. Notes, as a rule, are given in English, and in smaller letters, indenting like title. S. C. 21, 47, 53, 79.

Proper use of a terse, clear note is one mark of a good cataloger. Any fact should be noted which is necessary for adequate description of the book, either as a publication or as a particular copy; e. g. explanations of misleading or ambiguous titles, imperfections, etc.

If the title-page does not show it, state language of book, in a note; e. g. 'In French.'

Inclusiv dates for period coverd in history and travel are very useful and may be given in a note, or as part of the subject heading.

7 Subject entries

7a Main entry. Make a subject entry for main subject of each book. S. C. 3, 16, 19, 33, 64, 69.

Certain classes of books usually have no subject entry in a dictionary catalog; e. g. fiction, poetry and drama by a single author, general periodicals, autobiografy, etc. See Cutter, *Rules*, §92, 122.

In both dictionary and clast catalogs, make added entries for all other important subjects in which the book as a whole may be useful. S. C. 65, 70.

7b Analytic. Make subject analytics for distinct, important parts of books, 2t. For form of imprint see 5k. S. C. 44-46, 66, 71.

7c Pamflets. Independent books or pamflets are often bound in one volume. Catalog each independently; i. e. make subject and author cards, and added entries if necessary for each book or pamflet.

Put accession number on back of main card for first pamflet.

To both author and subject cards for all pamflets add note; e. g. 'Bound with other pamflets,' 'Bound with Shairp, J: C. Robert Burns.'

To trace entries, write on back of main author card the number of other sets of cards in the book, giving number of sets under each different author; e. g.

2 sets under Gray, T:
1   "   White, H: K.

On back of author card for each secondary pamflet write subject headings (dictionary catalog) or class numbers (clast catalog) relating to that pamflet.

8 Indention, spacing, call numbers

Indention

8a Author. Begin author's name at left red line, and succeeding lines of author's name at right red line. S. C. 1, etc.

8b Title. Write title on first blank line after author's name, or in case of anonymous book on second line of card, beginning at right red line. Begin succeeding lines at left red line. S. C. 1, 15, 22, 49, 56-57, etc.

8c Periodical, cyclopedia. Begin a periodical or cyclopedia on top line of card at right red line, indenting like ordinary title. S. C. 47, 49.

8d Subject heading. Write subject heading in red ink on top line of card beginning first and succeeding lines at right red line, followd by author's name indented as in 8a. S. C. 3, 16, 19, 64-66, etc.

Divisions of main subject may be indicated by underlining in a card catalog (S. C. 64-65, 67) and by italics in a printed catalog; e. g. England. *History.* If preferd, a dash [—] may be used to separate main and subordinate parts of subject heading, following analogy of 3j; e. g. England—History.

8e Added entry for editor, translator, title, etc. Write name of editor, translator, etc. on top line beginning at right red line, indenting as for subject heading, 8d. Begin author's name on next line after heading, indenting as in 8a. S. C. 2, 6, 29.

8f Analytic. Begin name of author of analytic at left red line indenting as in 8a. Begin title of analytic at right red line indenting as in 8b. S. C. 40, 43-46, 66, 71.

8g Reference. Write name from which reference is made, on top line, indenting as for subject heading, 8d. Write name to which reference i. made, on next line, indenting as for author heading, 8a. S. C. 7-14, 48.

'See' and 'see also' references in a dictionary catalog are indented like name references. S. C. 59-61.

If preferd, the words 'see' and 'see also' may be underlined.

When reference is made from one heading to several others, each of the headings to which reference is made is begun at the left red line. S. C. 60.

8h Note. Usually begin a note on second line after imprint, indenting like title, 8b. S. C. 21, 47, 53, 79.

8i Contents and series. Usually begin contents on second line after imprint, see S. C. 5. Give two lines to each entry on series card and keep all entries to right of right red line. Put volume or series numbers, if they occur, between red lines. S. C. 34, 36.

8j Extra card. When more space is needed, number and tie on extra cards and indent them as if all were on one card. Put call number on each card; see also 2u. S. C. 34, 47.

Spacing

8k Heading. Leave space of 1 cm in heading, between author's name and words or dates affixt; e. g. Jardine, Sir William, bart. ed. S. C. 6 7, 12, 20, 62.

8l Title and imprint. Leave also 1 cm between title and imprint, between three groups of imprint, and between date and series note, or other matter following date on same line; but leave no space if it would come at beginning of line. S. C. 1, 5, 30, 32, etc.

Leave same space in similar places on all added entry cards.

Call numbers

8m Position, etc. Write call number of every book, in blue ink, on all its cards; class number in upper left corner and under it the book number. Add volume number to all cards referring to only part of a set. S. C. 1-5, 15-19, 46, 49, etc.

All letters in call number should be printed not written, except where printed form may be confused with a figure, in which case the script form should be used; e. g. lower case l is liable to be mistaken for figure one, b for 6.

Reference cards have no call number.

Call numbers may be in red ink, if preferd; but in a clast catalog if red is used for call numbers, added subject numbers should be in blue. See 11b.

9 Arrangement

9a Order. Alfabet in order of English alfabet.

9b Umlaut. In a heading always write German ae, oe, ue, as ä, ö, ü, e. g. Müller, not Mueller, unless the other form is decidedly better known, e. g. Goethe, not Göthe. S. C. 9-10.

Arrange umlauted vowels as a, o, u; but in case of several surnames which are alike except umlaut, arrange umlauted after simple letter; e. g. all Müllers after all Mullers, W. Muller coming before A. Müller.

9c Person, place, title. Names of persons precede similar names of places, and places precede titles; e. g.
    Washington, George.
    Washington (D. C.)
    Washington Adams in England. (Title of book)

9d Surname. Surnames when used alone precede the same names with forenames; initials of forenames precede fully written forenames beginning with same initials; e. g. Brown; Brown, J. L.; Brown, James.

9e Prefix. Prefixes M' and Mc, S., St, Ste, Messrs, Mr and Mrs, arrange as if written in full, Mac, Sanctus, Saint, Sainte, Messieurs, Mister and Mistress.

9f Works. Works of an author arrange thus:
    1 Complete works
    2 Partial works
    3 Single works

Two or more works under the title of the first should be arranged with single works.
Arrange translations of an individual work directly after the original.
  4 Work as joint author
  5 Work as editor, translator, etc. (Added entries)

9g Country, city, society, etc. The following examples illustrate arrangement of headings for official bodies and names of institutions, etc. beginning with name of place, see 3j:

N. Y. (city)—Health, Board of.
N. Y. (county)—Finance dep't.
N. Y. (state)—Forest commission.
New York academy of medicine.
New York city charity organization society.
New York comic almanack.
New York county agricultural society.
New York dramatic news.
New York state tract society.
Newark (N. J.)—Common council.

9h Alfabeting. For farther details of alfabetic arrangement, see Cutter, *Rules*, §213-58.

10 Dictionary catalog

10a Subject headings. For rules for subject headings, see Cutter, *Rules*, p. 45-60.

For form of subject headings, follow A. L. A. *List of subject headings for use in dictionary catalogs*, 1898.

Write subject headings in red ink. The words 'see,' 'see also,' etc. may be written in black ink, if proferd. S. C. 59 61.

10b Sample cards. For sample cards for subject headings, see S. C. 3, 16, 19, 33, 44, 46, 59-61, 64-66.

10c Arrangement. For arrangement of a dictionary catalog, see Cutter, *Rules*, p. 83-98, also *Catalog 'A. L. A.' library*, p. 261-582.

10d Record of subject headings. Note briefly in the lower right corner on back of main card all the subject headings chosen for the book. S. C. 67.

11 Clast catalog

11a Subject entry. The subject is shown by class number in upper left corner of each card. S. C. 4, 15, 17, 69-72, etc. When necessary, as in a biografy, autobiografy, bibliografy, criticism, local history, genealogy, etc. additional subordinate headings are written in red ink at top of card. S. C. 33, 46, 74-80.

For fulness of author's name on subject card see 3b.

On main subject card a fuller title than that on main author card may sometimes be used to advantage. See 4a. S. C. 69.

Imprint, including series note, is the same as on main author card. See 5a-j. S. C. 4, 68-69.

Simplified Card Catalog Rules 27

11b Added subject number. Added subject numbers are written in red ink on fourth and succeeding lines of main subject card. S. C. 69. Class number for each added subject card is written in red ink on the top line of its card with call number directly below it. See 8m. S. C. 45-46, 70-71.
Only call numbers (never added subject numbers) are put on face of cards in name catalog. S. C. 68.

11c Bible. Enter *Bible* or any part of it including the *Apocrypha* under editor, translator, etc.; e. g. enter Alford, Henry, ed. *Greek testament with revised text*, under Alford; or, if there is no editor or translator, under first word of title like an anonymous book (2e); e. g. *Riverside parallel Bible*. S. C. 72.

Make references in name catalog to subject catalog for such headings as *Bible*, *Old testament*, *New testament*, and for names of single books of the *Bible* when the library contains separate editions of these. It is unnecessary to duplicate in the name catalog the group under 220 (*Bible*) and its subdivisions in the subject catalog. S. C. 73.

11d Biografy: clast catalog. In individual biografy write full name of biografee in red ink on top line of subject card, followd by subject entry for book in usual form. S. C. 33, 46. For arrangement see 11k.

In autobiografy the name is repeated, as author and biografee are the same (S. C. 74); e. g.

92   *Mill, John Stuart.*
M64   Mill, J: S.
        Autobiography.   O.   N. Y. 1873.

Collectiv biografy has usual form of subject card without a red ink heading.

When *Abridged decimal classification* is used, individual biografy is readily recognized by class number 92. Individual biografy of a special subject is clast with the subject in the following cases:

220.9 lives of Bible characters
326   "   slaves
397   "   gipsies
970.2   "   indians

11e Biografy: name catalog. If biografee cards are included in name catalog, they should be like the biografee subject card except that red ink numbers should be omitted. S. C. 33, 46. For arrangement see 11l. For use of colord cards, see 12.

11f Author bibliografy. Author bibliografy (clast in 012) is catalogd exactly like biografy. See 11c. S. C. 33, 46. For arrangement in name catalog, see 11l. For use of colord cards, see 12.

11g General criticism. Write in red ink on top line the name of person criticized (for fulness of name see 3b), followd by usual subject entry for author, title, etc. of book catalogd. Write in black ink, in small letters above red ink heading 'Criticism of'. S. C. 75. For arrangement of these cards, see 11k. For use of colord cards, see 12.

Make a duplicate of subject card for insertion in name catalog, but give name on top line in full (3a) and omit all added subject numbers. S. C. 76. For arrangement, see 11l. For use of colord cards, see 12.

General criticism is here used to include all criticism of an author's writings when such criticism is not confind to a special book.

11h Criticism of an individual work. Write cards the same as for general criticism, but add in red ink on second line a short title of work criticized. For arrangement, see 11k-l. For use of colord cards see 12, S. C. 77-78.

11i Genealogy. Make card for genealogy of a family in same form as for individual biografy, writing family name in red ink on the top line; e. g. Wheeler family. S. C. 79.

11j Local history. For history of a special town or county write name of town or county in red ink on top line, as a subject heading. S. C. 80

11k Arrangement: clast catalog. Arrange subject cards: 1) by class numbers, 2) by authors. If subordinate red ink headings are used, arrange: 1) by class numbers, 2) by red ink headings, 3) by authors. Criticism cards are arranged next after works criticized.

For description of the *Relativ subject index* used with a clast catalog arranged by the *Decimal classification*, see *Abridged decimal classification*, p. 7-8, 75-192; or for fuller statement see *Decimal classification*, pref. p. 10-12, p. 403-593.

11l Arrangement: name catalog. Arrange cards in name catalog as follows:

    1 bibliografy
    2 biografy
    3 general criticism of an author
    4 complete works
    5 partial works
    6 single works

Two or more works under the title of the first should be arranged with single works.

Arrange translations and criticisms of an individual work directly after the original.

    7 work as joint author
    8 work as editor, translator, etc.

Instead of white cards for biografy, bibliografy and criticism, colord cards may be used. See 12.

12 Colord cards

To make certain class of entries more prominent, either in a dictionary or a clast catalog, distinctiv colors may be used. In accordance with

this principle, green may be used for the biografy card described in
11e; blue for the bibliografy card in the name catalog, 11f; and canary
for the criticism card, 11g-h. For greater convenience they are prepared
with printed headings, 'For biography of,' 'For bibliography of,' 'For
criticism of,' and when so used, the word 'see' should be written in
black ink, 1 cm after red ink heading. S. C. 77-78.

Sample cards illustrating catalog rules

In the following illustrations, subject cards are markt (dictionary catalog), (clast catalog). Unless otherwise specified, all the other cards may be used in either a dictionary or a clast catalog.

Subject headings (S. C. 3, 16, 19, 33, 44, 46, 50-62, 64-66, 74-80), added subject numbers (S. C 45-46, 69-71), and number of copies (S. C. 63-66, 68-71) printed here in italics, should be written in red ink on the cards.

Small italics in imprint (S. C. 47) and in note (S. C. 53) indicate that the matter thus printed is to be written in pencil.

All the cards are P size (7.5 x 12.5 cm).

---

1 Main author card.   1c, 2a, 3a, 4a, 5a-b, 8a b, l-m

914.21
H2 Hare, Augustus J. C.
      Walks in London.   2v. in 1, illus. D.   N. Y.
   1878

---

2 Title card.   2s, 3c, 5b, 8c, l-m

914.21
H2 Walks in London.   1878
   Hare, A: J. C.

3 Subject card (dictionary catalog) 3b, 5b, 7a, 8d, 1-m

914.21   *London*
H2   Hare, A: J. C.
              Walks in London.   2v. in 1, illus. D.
         N. Y. 1878

4 Subject card (clast catalog) 3b, 5b, 7a, 11a

914.21   Hare, A: J. C.
H2   Walks in London.   2v. in 1, illus. D.
         N. Y. 1878

5 Author card with translator. 1c, 2a, 4b
           Contents. 6a, 8i

851   Dante Alighieri
D1   Divine comedy; tr. by H: W. Longfellow.
         3v. D.   Bost. 1871
              Contents
              v. 1 Inferno
              v. 2 Purgatorio
              v. 3 Paradiso

6 Translator card. 2r, 3c, 5b

851   Longfellow, Henry Wadsworth,   tr.
D1   Dante Alighieri
              Divine comedy.   1871.   3v.

7 Name reference: nobleman. 2o, v. 3c, 8g. k

         Disraeli, Benjamin,   see
         Beaconsfield, Benjamin Disraeli,   earl of

8 Name reference: compound name. 2v, 3c, r, 8g

Quiller-Couch, Arthur Thomas, see
Couch, Arthur Thomas Quiller-

9 Name reference: umlaut. 2v, 3c, 8g, 9b

Baedeker, Karl, see
Bädeker, Karl

10 Name reference: umlaut. 2v, 3c, 8g, 9b

Göthe, Johann Wolfgang von, see
Goethe, Johann Wolfgang von

11 Name reference: prefix. 2v, 3:l

Von
For names beginning with this prefix, see the latter part of the name.

12 Name reference: prefix. 2v, 3d, 8g, k

DeKalb, Johann, baron, see
Kalb, Johann, baron de

13 Name reference: well known anonymous classic. 2m, v

Reynard, see
Renard the fox

14 Title reference. 2s, v

Hamlet, see
Shakspere, William

32 Simplified Library School Rules

15 Anonymous book: author not found. 2e, 8b
Anonymous book (clast catalog) 2e, 7a, 11a

917.47
G7
    Greater New York album; 100 views. illus.
 S. Chic. 1895

16 Anonymous book (dictionary catalog) 2e, 7a, 8d

917.47
G7
    New York (city)

    Greater New York album; 100 views. illus.
 S. Chic. 1895

17 Added edition. 4h
Anonymous book: author found. 2e
Anonymous book: author found (clast catalog) 7a, 11a

808
B9
 Burgh, James
    Art of speaking. Ed. 2. D. Lond.
 1768

808
B9a
 —— —— S. Danbury, Ct. 1795

18 Added edition. 4h
Anonymous book: author found. Title card. 2e, 8e

808
B9
    Art of speaking. 1768
 Burgh, James

808
B9a
 —— —— 1795

Simplified Card Catalog Rules 33

19 Added edition. 4h
Anonymous book, author found (dictionary catalog) 2c, 7a

808
B9
    Elocution
    Burgh, James
        Art of speaking.   Ed. 2.   D.   Lond.
1768

808
B9a
    ——   S.   Danbury, Ct. 1795

20 Main entry under editor. 2a, 8k

973
qW
    Winsor, Justin,   ed.
        Narrative & critical history of America.   8v.
illus. maps, Q.   Bost. ʳ1884–89

21 Initials: main entry. 2b, 5i-j, 6b, 8h

245
W
    W,   M.
        Easter bells.   S.   n.p. n.d.

        Booklet

22 Initials: entry under real name. 1d, 2b

244
T8
    Tucker, Charlotte Maria
        Giant-killer; or, The battle which all must fight,
by A. L. O. E.   S.   N. Y. 1881

23 Reference from initials to real name. 2b, 8g

    E, A. L. O.   see
Tucker, Charlotte Maria

24 Reference from first initial to real name 2b, 8g

B86

A. L. O. E.   see
Tucker, Charlotte Maria

25 Pseudonymous book: entry under real name. 1d, 2a, c

Brontë, Charlotte
    Jane Eyre, an autobiography; ed. by Currer Bell.
D.   N. Y. 1857

26 Reference from pseudonym to real name. 2c, 8g

Bell, Currer,   pseud.   see
Brontë, Charlotte

27 Pseudonymous book: entry under pseudonym. 2c

817
T9

Twain, Mark,   pseud.
    Adventures of Huckleberry Finn.   illus. O.
N. Y. 1886

28 Reference from real name to pseudonym. 2c, 8g

Clemens, Samuel Langhorne,   see
Twain, Mark,   pseud.

29 Partial title. 2c, s, 8e

817
T9

Huckleberry Finn.   1886
Twain, Mark,   pseud.

30 Joint author: main entry. 2f

612
H9

Huxley, Thomas H. & Youmans, W: J.
    Elements of physiology & hygiene ; a text-book.
New ed.   illus. D.   N. Y. 1880

Simplified Card Catalog Rules 35

31 Joint author added entry 2f

612
H9
Youmans, William Jay & Huxley, T: H.
   Elements of physiology & hygiene.   1880

32 Biografy: main author entry. 2a
      Series note. 2n

92
P74
Woodberry, George E.
   Edgar Allan Poe.   D.   Bost. 1885.
   (American men of letters)

33 Biografy (dictionary catalog) 7a, 10a; (clast catalog) 11a, d; (name catalog) 11e, 12

92
P74
   Poe, Edgar Allan
Woodberry, G: E.
   Edgar Allan Poe.   D.   Bost. 1885
   (American men of letters)

34 Series: title entry. 2n, 8j
      Extra card. 8j

American men of letters ; ed. by C: D. Warner

92
W38
Scudder, H. E.   Noah Webster.   1882

92
I72
Warner, C: D.   Washington Irving.   1882

92
C77
Lounsbury, T: R.   James Fenimore Cooper.
   1883

92
F96
Higginson, T: W.   Margaret Fuller Ossoli.
   1889

92
P97
Woodberry, G: E.   Edgar Allan Poe.   1885

See next card

92
C97
    Cary, Edward. George William Curtis. 1894

    35 Reference from editor to title of series. 2u-v, 8g

    Morley, John,   ed.   see
English men of letters

    36 Series: editor entry. 2u

  Arber, Edward,   ed.
   English reprints.

821
M6z
  no. 8 Addison, Joseph. Criticism on Milton's Paradise lost.   1868

821
J2
  no. 19 James 1, king of England. Essayes of a prentise.   1895

    37 Reference from title of series to editor. 2u, 8g

   English reprints,   see
Arber, Edward,   ed.

    38 Forename: main entry. 2q, 40
      Series note. 2u

821
J2
 James 1, king of England
  Essayes of a prentise in the divine art of poesie,
Edin. 1585; A counterblaste to tobacco, Lond. 1604.
S.   Westminster 1895.   (Arber, Edward,   ed.
English reprints. no. 19)

Simplified Card Catalog Rules 37

39 Book containing analytic by same author, publisht separately. 2t

J27d James, Henry
　　　Daisy Miller; & an International episode.
　　illus. O.　　N. Y. 1893

40 Author analytic. 2t, 5k, 8f

J27d James, Henry
　　　International episode.　(in his Daisy Miller.
　　1893.　p.135)

41 Title analytic. 2t

J27d International episode
　　James, Henry.　(in his Daisy Miller.　1893.　p.135)

42 Book containing analytic by different author. 2f, t, 5c

811 Cary, Alice
C3　　　Poetical works of Alice & Phœbe Cary.
　　illus. O.　Bost. 1891.　(Household ed.)

43 Author analytic. 2f, t

811 Cary, Phœbe
C3　　　Poems.　(in Cary, Alice.　Poetical works.
　　1891.　p.187)

44 Subject analytic, separate title-page (dictionary catalog) 2t, 4e, 5k, 7b, 8f

917.48　　New Jersey
T4　　Thomas, Gabriel
　　　Historical description of West-New-Jersey.
　　D.　Lond. 1698.　(in his Historical account of
　　Pensilvania.　1848)

45 Subject analytic: separate title-page (clast catalog) 2t, 4e, 5k, 7b, 8f, 11b

917.49
917.48
T4

Thomas, Gabriel
 Historical description of West-New-Jersey.
D.   Lond. 1698.   (in his Historical account of Pensilvania. 1848)

46 Biografic analytic (dictionary catalog) 2t, 5k, 7b, 8f; (name catalog) 11e
 Biografic analytic (clast catalog) 11b, d
Omit added subject number in red for both dictionary and name catalogs

92
821
H53
v. 1

Herbert, George
Walton, Izaak
 Life of Mr George Herbert.   (in Herbert, George. Works. 1846. v.1, pref. p.1)

47 Periodical: changed title. 2j, 5e, 8c
 Extra card. 8j

051
C3

Century illustrated monthly magazine.   illus. O.
N. Y. °1871-*date*
 Library has:
  v.1-22   1870-81   v. 51-52   1895-96
            53-54   1896-97
  24-38   1882-89   55   1897-98

  46-50   1893-95   See next card

051
C3

2
1870-Oct. 1881, v. 1-22 pub. under title Scribner's monthly.

Simplified Card Catalog Rules

48 Periodical reference changed title. 2j, v, 8g

  Scribner's monthly, see
Century illustrated monthly magazine

     49 Cyclopedia 2k, 8c
      Index 4h

R032 Encyclopædia Britannica. Ed. 9.
qE5 24 v. illus. maps. Q. Edin. 1875-88
R032 —— Index. Q. Edin. 1889
qE5
v.o

R032 —— Supplement to 9th ed. 4 v. illus. Q.
qE5
v. 25-28 Phil. 1885-89

     50 Government department. 2d, 3g j
      Atlas. 5f-g

557.4 New Hampshire—Geological survey
qN Geology of New Hampshire ; a report. 3v.
 illus. maps, Q & atlas F°. Concord 1874-78
557.4 Atlas, F°
yN

     51 Government bureau. 2d, 3g
      Subordinate heading. 3j
      Inversion 3k

929.9 U. S.—Navigation, Bureau of
qU Flags of maritime nations. Ed. 5. illus.
 Q. Wash. 1882

52 Government department: reference. 3g
　　Subordinate heading. 3j
　　　Inversion. 3k

U. S.—Navy, Dep't of the,　　see also
U. S.—Naval observatory
U. S.—Navigation, Bureau of
U. S.—Naval academy, Annapolis

53 Society. 2d, j, 3i
　　Note. 5d, 6b, 8h

973
A5

American historical association
　　Papers.　5 v. O.　N. Y. 1886-91
　　v.4 wanting
　　No more publisht. Subsequent papers appear in the association's reports to congress.

54 Institution. 2d, h, 3i

019
qA

Ames free library, North Easton (Mass.)
　　Catalogue.　2 v. O.　Bost. 1883

55 Institution: reference from city. 3i
　　Inversion. 3k

North Easton (Mass.), Ames free library, see Ames free library, North Easton (Mass.)

56 Classic: author unknown. 2m, 4f

892
A6

Arabian nights' entertainments
　　Book of the thousand nights & one night; done into English by John Payne.　9 v. illus. O.　N. Y. 1884

57 Map. 2f, 5h

912
qF
French, F. F. & others
      Map of Orange & Rockland counties, N. Y. from
hetual surveys by F. F. French, W. E. Wood & S. N.
Beers.   108½ x 155½ cm F.   Phil. 1859

58 Title: omissions. Rule 4a
Original title

The ingenious gentleman Don Quixote of La Mancha by Miguel de Cervantes Saavedra,
done into English by Henry Edward Watts, a new edition with notes, original and selected,
in four volumes. London, Adam and Charles Black, 1895

The above title is abbreviated on the card as follows

C14 | Cervantes Saavedra, Miguel de
     | Don Quixote ; done into English by H: E: Watts.
     | New ed.   4 v. O.   Lond. 1895

59 Subject reference: 'see also' (dictionary catalog) 8g, 10a

          Moral philosophy,   see
Ethics

60 Subject reference: 'see' (dictionary catalog) 8g, 10a

          Education,   see also
Colleges & universities
Kindergarten
Public schools
University extension

61 General subject reference 'see also' (dictionary catalog) 8g, 10a

          Education   see also
Names of countries states, etc., under their subhead
Education

62 Bible (dictionary catalog) 2l, 4c

220.5
M3
Bible. Whole Bible. French
   (La) Sainte Bible; revue par David Martin.
Ed. 7.   D.   N. Y. 1896

63 Main author entry (dictionary catalog) 3a, 4i

942.04
qB
Brooke, Richard
   $_3$cop Visits to fields of battle in England of the 15th century; & papers on archaeological subjects.
maps, Q.   Lond. 1857

64 Subject entry (dictionary catalog) 7a, 4i, 8d

942.04
qB
   England. History
Brooke, Richard
   $_3$cop Visits to fields of battle in England of the 15th century.   maps, Q.   Lond. 1857

65 Added subject entry (dictionary catalog) 7a, 4i, 8d

942.04
qB
   England. Archeology
Brooke, Richard
   $_3$cop Visits to fields of battle in England of the 15th century ; & papers on archaeological subjects.   1857

66 Subject analytic (dictionary catalog) 4i, 5k, 7b

942.04
qB
   Firearms
Brooke, Richard
   $_3$cop On the general use of firearms by the English in the 15th century. (in his Visits to fields of battle in England. 1857. p.213)

Simplified Card Catalog Rules 43

67 Record of subject headings on back of main card   S. C. 63 (dictionary catalog)
    1f, 4i, 8d, 10d

```
                          O




 cop. 1
 cop. 2-3

                                      England.    History
 647                                     "        Archeology
 80g-10
                                      Firearms
```

---

68 Main author entry (clast catalog)   3a, 4i

| 942.04 | Brooke, Richard |
| qB | ₃ᶜᵒᵖ· Visits to fields of battle in England of the 15th century.   maps, Q.   Lond. 1857 |

---

69 Main subject entry: added subject numbers (clast catalog)   4i, 11a-b

942.04	Brooke, Richard
qB	₃ᶜᵒᵖ· Visits to fields of battle in England of the 15th
913.4	century; & papers upon archaeological subjects.
355	maps, Q. Lond. 1857

---

70 Added subject entry (clast catalog)   7a, 11b

913.4	Brooke, Richard
942.04	₃ᶜᵒᵖ· Visits to fields of battle in England of the 15th
qB	century; & papers on archaeological subjects. 1857

71 Subject analytic (clast catalog) 5k, 7b, 11b

355
942.04
qB

Brooke, Richard
On the general use of firearms by the English in the 15th century. (in his Visits to fields of battle in England. 1857. p.213)

72 Bible (clast catalog) 2e, l, 11c

220.5
qR

Riverside parallel Bible ; being King James's version arranged in parallel columns with the revised versions of 1881 & 1885.   Q.   Bost. 1885

73 Bible: reference from name catalog to clast catalog. 11c

Bible,   see
Subject catalog, 220–229

74 Autobiografy (clast catalog) 11d

92
A54

Andersen, Hans Christian
Andersen, H. C.
Story of my life ; now first tr. into English.   D.   N. Y. 1871

75 General criticism (clast catalog) 11g

S84z

Criticism of
Stevenson, R. L.
Raleigh, Walter
Robert Louis Stevenson.   D.   Lond. 1895

76 General criticism (name catalog) 11g

S84z   Criticism of
       Stevenson, Robert Louis
   Raleigh, Walter
       Robert Louis Stevenson.   D.   Lond. 1895

77 Criticism of an individual work: canary card (clast catalog) 11h, 12

941.5   For criticism of
F9z   Froude, J. A.
          Lectures on Ireland,   see
   Burke, Rev. T: N.
       Ireland's case stated in reply to Mr Froude.
   D.   N. Y. 1873

78 Criticism of an individual work: canary card (name catalog) 11h, 12

941.5   For criticism of
F9z   Froude, James Anthony
          Lectures on Ireland,   see
   Burke, Rev. T: N.
       Ireland's case stated in reply to Mr Froude.
   D.   N. Y. 1873

79 Genealogy (clast catalog) 11i

929   *Andrews family*
A5   Drummond, J. H.
       Henry Andrews of Taunton.   O.   Bost.
   1897

       Reprinted fr. New England historical & genealogical register for
   Oct. 1897.

80   Local history (clast catalog)   11j

974.7 **W4**	*Troy* Weise, A. J. History of the city of Troy. illus. maps, O. Troy, N. Y. 1876

SIMPLIFIED ACCESSION RULES

For a full discussion of the accession department, see A. L. A. *Papers prepared for the World's library congress*, 1896, p 809-26.

20 Accession book

20a Importance. First of all records to be fild, and by no means last in importance, is the accession book, the history of the growth of the library. To this the librarian turns for final reference in doubtful cases. Here is the complete story of each volume, fully told, but in the most compact form. It is the official indicator for the whole collection, the most permanent of library records. Each line is a separate pigeonhole, in which, if not exactly the book, all the condenst facts about the book are placed. Thence they are never removed, they are not stolen, or lent, or condemd, or withdrawn, or sent to the binder, or lost. The card is never misplaced, the entry does not mysteriously disappear, a new edition never supersedes, the entry never needs to be rewritten. The librarian may turn to his accession book to learn *what*, and *where*, and *when*, and *whence*, and *how much*, and feel sure of his answer. A well made accession book has an element of mathematical exactness unknown to the card catalog or shelf list. It is the *editio princeps*.

By this complete, unchangeable record the additions for every day, week, month, and year are shown at a glance; also the total number of volumes which the library has had, and its present number by subtracting the total withdrawn and lost.

20b Form. For this essential book many forms have been used, but the best features of all were finally combined in the *A L. A. standard accession book* made by a committee of experts who compared thuroly all the various forms collected, made and tested samples, and finally agreed on all details of materials, ruling, printing and binding.

To save expense, however, smaller libraries prefer the *Condensed accession book* described below and illustrated by the sample sheet facing p.52. On the left page of the *Condensed accession book* are accession number, author and title. On the right page are the regular imprint entries: place, publisher, year, pages and size followd by the description of the special copy, i. e. binding, source and cost. Next is given the call number composed of class, book and volume numbers, and finally a column for remarks, in which are added notes of changes, loss, rebinding, sale, etc.

By the rule of a line to a number, and dates in the left margin, every page has exactly 25 entries, and the eye is greatly helpt in quick reference. The red lines help the eye in passing across the page, following one or two above or below, and thus avoiding the danger of getting off the line in crossing the fold.

21 Reception

21a Bill. Arrange books in order of bill and check each item that is correct. Verify prices and footings of bill and certify bill with initials.

21b Order slip. Compare books with order slips taken from order index. Record date of receipt and cost price on order slips, and put each order slip in the corresponding book.

After accession numbers have been stampt on order slips (see 22f) file order slips in receipt index alfabeticly.

21c Book. Pencil date, source and price in cents on inner margin of first recto after the title page; e. g. 1 Je 98 Put. 167. See 22b.

21d Private mark. Put in private mark when entry is made in accession book.

Each library selects its own private mark. Some libraries use a pin hole always on the same page; e. g. 49 or 33 or 65. This should be a page in the first 100, that it may apply to thin books. Others choose a more complicated rule, less easily discoverd; e. g. the highest page made all of 3's, i. e. 3, 33, or 333, or the highest page in 1, 2, 3 order, i. e. 12, 123 or 1234. This perforation is a safe private mark, as it can hardly be found by accident or removed, if known, so as not to be detected by an expert.

22 Entry

22a Order. Enter on accession book in order of bill.

The official business record of additions should be kept as strictly up to date as a cash account. If more books come in than can be written up at once, and some are wanted in special haste, they may be enterd first, but under no circumstances should leave the library till properly added. Once bearing the accession number, other facts are readily found; but a book without this guide is easily lost or confused with books from other sources or coming in on other dates. The accession book corresponds to the invoice book of a business house.

22b Abbreviations, etc. Use the library abbreviations in all entries. See 52.

These include dates, authors' forenames, place, size, binding, etc. So many facts are given in so little space, that it is important to save room by using abbreviations; and as only those familiar with them use this book, the objection against the use of abbreviations in public catalogs does not hold good. All obvious contractions may be used in this book, specially in titles.

Each user should, before making the first entry, read these rules thru carefully and add neatly in manuscript any added rules that seem desirable, and a 'List of special abbreviations,' which will show names of agents, funds, etc. local in character, but occurring so often as to need contraction. This done, a glance will show what rule was decided on and explain any abbreviations not on the printed list.

22c Date of reception. Give day, month, and year in upper left margin of each left-hand page, and day and month (52i) before the first entry of each day.

The running date at the top is used in turning to find books by dates. It applies to all entries till a new date is prefixt to the accession number. If a whole page or more are receivd the same day, the date in top margin is enough. Some-

Simplified Accession Rules

times only a single book is added, but its date must be given as carefully as for a pageful, for dates, like other figures, are almost worthless if not exact. This date shows when the book came into the library, and, if the accessions were written up daily, it would also be the date of entry. A large number coming at once should be entered under the same date, to show that they came together, even if the entry takes several days.

If books accumulate they should be kept in order of reception, which is shown by date on inner margin of first recto, 21c; and if any are specially wanted before the others, the lines may be counted off so as to accession in proper order.

22d Accession number. Give to each volume the next consecutiv number on the first blank line of the accession book, and enter this number on the lower margin of the first recto, after the title page of each volume receivd. Never assign the same number to another volume, even if the original is lost, sold, exchanged, or condemnd and an exact duplicate obtaind.

An accession number is given to each separate volume, and not to works, sets, lots, series, or collections. Numbering *works*, in however many volumes they may chance to be, always leads to confusion. The last number should show how many volumes the library has receivd from the beginning.

The entries, if the same, are dittoed with labor too trifling for mention. One ditto mark serves for the whole line, instead of dittoing each word, and even this is done only once in the life of the book. The *Condensed accession book* has from 1000 to 5000 lines or pigeon-holes for as many distinct volumes. Trial of various plans proves it best to assign one of these pigion-holes or lines across the book to each volume. There is then no trouble in recording titles, imprint, cost, source, binding, etc., for the different volumes of a set. If any volume is lost, or rebound, or requires any note or comment to preserve its history and the record of its present state, the way is perfectly simple.

22e Number on book. As soon as assignd, stamp or write the accession number near the bottom of first recto after the title-page.

When the book is rebound, the number is thus preservd for immediate reference or identification.

22f Number on card, order slip and bill. Stamp or write the accession number on the back of main author card, crosswise of the back on the reverse of the upper left corner of the front (see *Simplified card catalog rules*, 1f S. C. 67) also on the order slip under 'Library no.' and after the first and last items on the bill.

This number on the card gives easy reference to the accession book. A card with an accession number on the back is recognized at a glance as a main card

In case of sets, give only first and last accession number when consecutive, e. g. 7523-4 2v.

The numbering stamp, tho costly at first, is a real economy in a library, where it saves its cost in time of assistants, besides giving compact printed numbers of the greatest legibility.

22g Pamflets. Pamflets not previously accessioned, when bound, are entered the same as new books, on the date when they come in from the bindery, which is the time of their reception as books. In the source column the abbreviation 'pam. bd.' meaning 'pamflet bound,' in place of the agent's name, shows that the pamflets had been in the library, but not enterd.

For a full discussion of pamflets see A L. A. *Papers prepared for the World's library congress*, 1896, p. 826-35.

22h Author. Write author's surname in the form used in the card catalog (*Simplified card catalog rules* 3a) and give only initials or colon abbreviations of forenames (52a) e. g. Fiske, J:; Barrie, J. M. Give only surnames of joint authors; e. g. Huxley & Youmans. See sample accession sheet facing p. 52.

The form used in the author column must correspond with the entry on the main card for the catalog, hence a careless heading should not be written here at the risk of error. If in doubt, leave the author column blank, and fill in after the heading is decided for the catalog.

The line separating author and title is faint, so as to be seen only when lookt for, to guide in making the titles line accurately one under the other. When author's name or the title is very long, this line is simply disregarded, but in most entries there will be a little space between the author and the beginning of the title.

If the work is anonymous, leave the author column blank, to be fild when authorship is discovered.

A volume of pamflets is enterd under the heading used on the main card for the first pamflet (*Simplified card catalog rules*, 7c) with a note in title column; e. g. '& 9 other pam.'

22i Title. Give only a brief title.

Other facts are given with so much fulness that the book is readily identified.

22j Imprint. Give place, date and size, in accordance with *Simplified card catalog rules* (5a, f, h-j), except that more abbreviations may safely be used. See also 22b, k-n, 52.

22k Place and publisher. If several places or publishers are printed, give only the first named on title-page, or the most important, if main publisher is given in large type with fine type names preceding.

Leave space between abbreviation for place and publisher, so entry will not look like a name and initials; e. g. L. Macmillan, *not* L. Macmillan.

22l Year. Give date of publication in arabic figures. Use copyright date only when there is no date on title-page. "1904 — pc1909.

22m Pages. Usually give main paging. If two groups of paging are about equal give both; if minor group contains more than 100 pages, give both.

For parts of books separately bound, give first and last pages; e. g. p. 613-1120.

In case of pamflet volumes give paging of first pamflet only.

22n Size. Except in rare books, the size letter is sufficient. See 52f.

22o Binding. Give binding material, indicating half-binding by prefixing ½ or better a superior²; e. g. ²mor. See 52j.

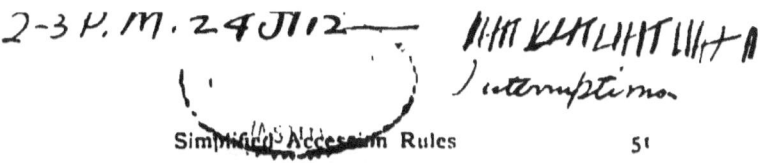

Simplified Accession Rules

22p Source. Under 'Source' write name of giver, if the book is a gift; name of firm or library agents of whom bought, and name of fund, if bought from income of a special fund.

The funds of each library are so well known to the librarian that initials are ample; the column for source allows room for both agent and fund

22q Cost. Under 'Cost' give in dollars and cents the actual cost of the book.

In case of foreign books convenience requires that cost be given in ordinary denominations, so that a moment suffices to tell an inquirer the cost of any book.

When several volumes of a set are bought at once, give cost of series opposit the first volume enterd, preceded by number of volumes included; e. g. v. 4, 5, and 6 of some work come in together, and cost together $13.34. Instead of dividing this up, and entering $4.48 against each volume, make the entry against the first (v. 4); e. g. 3 v. $13.44

Give items of cost carefully, thus making the accession book for all practical purposes the invoice book.

Mark gifts 'g' in cost column.

22r Call number. Enter class, book and volume numbers when assignd

Tho some libraries prefer to omit them, these numbers are of value in the accession book because: 1) They refer directly to the shelves and shelf list, 2) They are the best check to show that all books paid for really get on the shelves, instead of disappearing by accident or design before being enterd in the catalog and shelf list; 3) The class number makes analysis and statistics much easier.

Class and book number columns are left blank till the book is clast, catalogd and shelflisted, and are then fild in from the main card before it is put into the catalog.

For use of printed form of letters in call numbers see *Simplified card catalog rules*, 8m

22s Volume number. Give number of volume if more than one. It in only one volume, leave this column blank as 1 indicates that it is the first of a set of two or more.

In the volume column, enter two volumes bound in one 1-2, 3-4, etc Enter one volume bound in two parts 1¹, 1², etc. each part on a separate line.

Make all entries of facts perfectly definit.

22t Second copy. When two or more copies of a book are preservd write 'cop. 1' and 'cop. 2' in volume column. If a volume number i in volume column, write 'cop. 1' or 'cop. 2' above.

22u Remarks. Under 'Remarks' indicate any rebinding, sale, loss, exchange, withdrawal as duplicate, binding in with another volume, or any change or disposition.

The preceding entries tell what the book was when it came into the library. 'Remarks tell of any changes, and of the final disposition in case the book is no longer in its accustomd place. This rule requires less labor than at first appears, and saves more than it costs. When books come in from the bindery, it is a very brief matter to open to their numbers, and note the new binding with its cost

Then if the volume is lost and the reader is required to pay for it, there is a means of knowing whether it was in paper as at first bought for 25 cents, or in half morocco as rebound, at an added cost of $1. The accession book is the book of final reference for these technical facts that do not appear in the catalog or shelf list. The efficient librarian must be able somewhere to refer to everything of the kind, and for this no other record offers so great advantages.

22v Pictures, statuary, maps, etc. Enter on a separate accession book, pictures, statuary, maps, and all articles, other than books, added to the library. Record date, source, cost, and any other items of interest.

To distinguish works of art and their numbers from books, prefix A, marking the first work of art A_1, and so on, the last number showing the extent of the collection. If wisht, a similar list for scientific specimens can be made under S_1, for maps under M_1, etc.

Maps, charts, etc. not in book form, should be stampt in lower right corner, or near title. In size column, give length and breadth in centimeters; e. g 41 x 52 cm.

23 Stamping, plating, pocketing and labeling

See also *Catalog of 'A. L. A' library*, 1893, pref p 17-19

23a Stamping. Stamp each full title page in every book on upper right corner.

Stamp the first page of text proper (i. e. matter after preface or introduction) in upper right corner.

Stamp all plates and maps not included in paging. Do not stamp illustrations included in text.

On plates, portraits, etc. stamp margin and a little of picture, but take great care not to disfigure picture by stamping on an important part. e. g. face of a portrait.

When an embossing stamp is used and there are several plates, maps, etc. in a volume, emboss at different distances from top of page to avoid spreading the book.

If plates are so numerous that embossing will swell the book materially, or if plates are on too heavy paper for perforating or embossing stamps, use ink stamp (small type) on face of plate.

23b Plating. Paste bookplate in center of inside of front cover. If this space is occupied by another bookplate, autograf or matter of value, place plate above or below, as there may be room. If there is not blank space enough for plate, paste its edge on inside edge of cover.

23c Pocketing. If book pockets are used, paste them in center of inside of back cover, with opening toward the inner edge.

23d Labeling or gilding. For methods of marking books see *Library notes*, v. 3, no. 11, p. 426-28.

Source	Cost		Class	Book	Vol.	REMARKS
pub	g		973	F5		
„	„			H39m		
Put.	2		973.7	D6		lost 150 Ag 96, repl. by 72
„	1		204	W3		
author	g		973.7	R3		2cl. binder
S Put.			67 917.47	G7		
„			84	C88w		
K.Y.M.A.	1		883	H7		
pub.	3v.	9	851	D1	1	
„			„	„	2	
„			„	„	3	
„			210	J27d		
S L.S.	g	60	929.9	qU		
,S Put.		34	973.7	B4		bd. 2 no. 9096
pub.		25				2D96 to W.B. 50c. dup. 30 N96 sold.
Dowling		80	817	T96		
Put.		83	92	F83		
O sam. bd.			304	C2		
K. Jones	g		612	H9		
pub.		40	821	G7		
O Put.			84	F85m		
„	2		973.7	D6		repl. 53
„	2 cop.	2		B27s cop.1		
				„ cop2		

26	Fiske, J.	Hist of U.S. for schools	B.	Houghton 1895	553 D	"no pub."	g	973	F5	
27	Hawthorne, N.	Marble faun	"	1888	206 "	cl "			H39m	
28	Dodge, J.A.	Bird's-eye view of our civil war	"	Osgood 1884	346 O	" Put.	2	973.7	D6	by 72 lost 150g 96 r4
29	Watson, J.M.	Mind of the Master	N.Y.	Dodd 1896	338 D	" "	1	204	W3	
30	Reeves, J.J.	Hist. of 24ch. N.J. vol.	Camden	Chew 1889	45 O	paperwhor	g	973.7	R3	ich. binder
31		Greater N.Y. album	Ch.	Rand 1895	104 S	cl Put.	67	917.47	G7	
32	Craddock, C.E.	Where the battle was fought	B.	Osgood 1884	423 D	" "		84	C88w	
33	Homer	Iliad. Buckley, tr.	L.	Bohn 1851	466 "	ref ex. Y.M.C.	1	883	H7	
34	Dante Alighieri	Divine comedy Longfellow, tr.	B.	Houghton 1891	446 "	cl pub.	3v.	9 851	D1	1
35	"	"	"	"	440 "	" "		"	"	2
36	"	"	"	"	450 "	" "		"	"	3
37	James, H.	Daisy Miller & an Internat. episode	N.Y.	Harper 1893	234 O	" "		210	J27d	
38	U.S.-Navigation, Bureau of Flags of maritime nations		W.	Gov't 1882	7 Q	" U.S.	g	60 929.9	gU	
39	Beecher, H:W.	Speeches on the rebellion	N.Y.	Lovell 1887	366 D	pap Put.		34 973.7	B4	bd no 3096
40	Adams, H.B.	Norman constables in Amer.	Balt.	J.H. univ 1883	38 O	" pub.		25	.	
41	Twain, Mark	Adventures of Huckleberry Finn	N.Y.	Webster 1886	366 "	cl Dowling		80 817	T96	2D96 to W B. & dup 307.96 sold
42	Morse, J.J.	B: Franklin (Amer. statesmen)	B.	Houghton 1889	428 D	" Put.		83 92	F83	
43	Carey, H.C.	Credit system in France, Gr. Br. & U.S. & other.	Ph.	Carey 1838	130 O	pam "no pam bd.		304	C2	
44	Huxley & Youmans	Elements of physiology & hygiene	N.Y.	Appleton 1880	485 D	" J.K. Jones		612	H9	
45	Gray, J.	Selected poems	Ox.	Clar. pr. 1892	156 "	bds pub.		40 821	G7	
46	Frederic, H.	March hares	N.Y.	Appleton 1896	281 S	cl Put.		84	F85m	
47	Dodge, J.A.	Bird's-eye view of our civil war	B.	Osgood 1884	346 O	" "	2	973.7	D6	repl 53
48	Barrie, J.M.	Sentimental Tommy	N.Y.	Scribner 1896	478 D	" "	2cop 2		B27s	cop 1
49	"	"	"	"	" "	" "			"	cop 2
50		Century N 95- Ap 96	"	Century "	960 O	"mor sh bd		051	C3	51

SIMPLIFIED BOOK NUMBERS

For a full discussion of book numbers see *Library notes*, v. 3, no. 11: 119-50.

30 Arrangement of books in each class. The following rules assume that the books in a library have been separated into classes in some form of relativ location and that a distinguishing mark or number has been given to each book to designate its class. For convenience, the class numbers of the *Abridged decimal classification* are used in illustration. For definition of class number see p.7.

For fiction, which is the largest class in most popular libraries, the class number should be omitted altogether. Thus absence of any class number shows that the book belongs to the class fiction.

After books have been separated into their various classes, there may be in some cases two, in others 200 or more volumes, all bearing the same class number. If there is no arrangement in the class, much time is wasted in finding books. In small classes a particular book may be pickt out at a glance, but in large classes all the titles may have to be read in succession till the one wanted is reacht. It is very important, therefore, that the various books of each class be arranged in some definit order. For popular libraries, an alfabetic arrangement, usually by authors, is best.

31 Book numbers

For definition of book number see p.7.

31a Purpose. In order that books may be quickly and accurately placed, calld for, found and charged there should be given to each book, except fiction (see 30), both a class number and a book number. The book number distinguishes each book from every other in the same class, and in combination with the class and volume number distinguishes each volume from every other in the library. Without book numbers, it takes longer both to find and replace books, and there is great danger of putting them in wrong places, as publishers' bindings can not be depended on as a guide.

Books in each class should be placed on the shelves in the exact alfabetic and numeric order of the book numbers.

The call number (the combination of the class and book number, see definition p. 7) should be placed both on the back of the book and on the bookplate inside the front cover. See *Simplified accession rules*, 23b, d. No book should be lent till plainly markt with its call number.

31b Principles. Three tests to be applied to any system of book numbers are, simplicity, brevity and utility (i. e. capacity to serve some purpose beside that of an arbitrary mark).

Book numbers should be so simple as to be readily written without mistakes by readers ignorant of the library system and easily understood by unskild assistants who must get and replace the books.

SIMPLIFIED BOOK NUMBERS

For a full discussion of book numbers see *Library notes*, v. 3, no. 11: 119-50.

30 Arrangement of books in each class. The following rules assume that the books in a library have been separated into classes in some form of relativ location and that a distinguishing mark or number has been given to each book to designate its class. For convenience, the class numbers of the *Abridged decimal classification* are used in illustration. For definition of class number see p. 7.

For fiction, which is the largest class in most popular libraries, the class number should be omitted altogether. Thus absence of any class number shows that the book belongs to the class fiction.

After books have been separated into their various classes, there may be in some cases two, in others 200 or more volumes, all bearing the same class number. If there is no arrangement in the class, much time is wasted in finding books. In small classes a particular book may be pickt out at a glance, but in large classes all the titles may have to be read in succession till the one wanted is reacht. It is very important, therefore, that the various books of each class be arranged in some definit order. For popular libraries, an alfabetic arrangement, usually by authors, is best.

31 Book numbers

For definition of book number see p. 7.

31a Purpose. In order that books may be quickly and accurately placed, calld for, found and charged there should be given to each book, except fiction (see 30), both a class number and a book number. The book number distinguishes each book from every other in the same class, and in combination with the class and volume number distinguishes each volume from every other in the library. Without book numbers, it takes longer both to find and replace books, and there is great danger of putting them in wrong places, as publishers' bindings can not be depended on as a guide.

Books in each class should be placed on the shelves in the exact alfabetic and numeric order of the book numbers.

The call number (the combination of the class and book number, see definition p. 7) should be placed both on the back of the book and on the bookplate inside the front cover. See *Simplified accession rules*, 23b, d. No book should be lent till plainly markt with its call number.

31b Principles. Three tests to be applied to any system of book numbers are, simplicity, brevity and utility (i. e. capacity to serve some purpose beside that of an arbitrary mark).

Book numbers should be so simple as to be readily written without mistakes by readers ignorant of the library system and easily understood by unskild assistants who must get and replace the books.

They should also be as short as possible to keep at a minimum the clerical work to which even a single unnecessary character for each book adds perceptibly.

They should give as much added information as possible. The most useful book number is some substitute for a name, distinct, easy to read, easy to write.

31c **Form.** The best form for this substitute for a name is a capital letter followd by arabic figures.

For use of printed form of letters in call numbers see *Simplified card catalog rules*, 8m.

32 Arrangement by use of tables

32a **Cutter tables.** The best and most widely used translation system for names is that devized by Mr C: A. Cutter. This system should be used wherever a more exact alfabetic arrangement is desired than that described in 37.

These tables represent a name by its initial followd by figures used decimally (to allow intercalation) and so cast off as to keep the names in almost strict alfabetic order. In these tables the first few letters of the most common surnames are given in columns in exact alfabetic order. In parallel columns, opposite each combination, is its translation into figures to which the initial letter of the name must be prefixt.

The first edition of the tables carried the subdivisions to two figures; in the second edition entitled *Alfabetic-order tables altered and fitted with three figures by Kate E. Sanborn*, the numbers are carried to three figures. The later edition has been used in the following rules.

32b **Author arrangement.** Usually assign book number from author. For treatment of individual biografy see 35a-d. See also 34c-d, 36a.

32c **Length of number.** Use initial of author and first figure of number except in fiction and individual biografy when two figures from the tables should be used; e. g.

    Dickens, Charles. Child's history of England   942
                                                                                 D5
          "   Barnaby Rudge   D54
          "   Collection of letters   92
                                                                              D54

See also 32d-e, 34b, 35b.

32d **Extra figure.** Add a figure from the tables to the book number, when necessary to distinguish different authors in the same class; e. g.
        Aldrich, A. R.   811
                              A3
        Aldrich, T: B.   811
                              A36

Simplified Book Numbers 55

32e Large book. For books larger than octavo in all classes, use initial only, unless an added figure is needed to distinguish, in which case the tables should be used.

Prefix size mark to the book number. Use q for books between 25 and 35 cm in hight, and f for books 35-50 cm, x for 50-70 cm, y for 70-90 cm and z for all books over 90 cm; e. g.

    Child. Spanish-American republics.   Q   918
                                                                           qC

In small libraries having very few books above q size, the books markt f, x, y and z may be kept together.

33 Title marks

33a Arrangement of titles. Arrange all titles of an author, in any given class, in alfabetic order as far as possible. For the first book add no mark for title unless there are likely to be many more books by the same author, in which case add a lower case letter for the first title. For subsequent books or for different editions add lower case initial of catch title; e. g.

Lowell, J. R.	Biglow papers. 1892	817 L.9
"	Meliboeus-Hipponax; the Biglow papers. 1848	817 L.9b
"	Fable for critics	817 L.9f

For treatment of second copy see 33d.

33b Titles with same initial. If two or more titles begin with the same initial, the second letter of the title may be added to distinguish all titles after the first; e. g.

Scott, Sir Walter.	Abbot	S43
"	Betrothed	S43b
"	Black dwarf	S43bl
"	Bride of Lammermoor	S43br

33c Titles beginning with same two letters. If two or more titles begin with the same two letters the added letter may be selected from each title so as to secure alfabetic order; e. g.

Barr, A. E.	Last of the Macallisters	B26l
"	Lone house	B26lo
"	Lost silver	B26ls
"	Love for an hour	B26lv

Arbitrary letters may also be used for this purpose.

33d Second copy. Distinguish different copies of the same book by calling the first book cop. 1, the second, cop. 2, etc.

In fiction treat different editions as different copies unless the edition is considerably alterd or abridged, in which case follow 33a; e. g.

R or Ref. for reference collection.

56   Simplified Library School Rules

  Defoe. [Life and adventures of] Robinson Crusoe. 1868 jD31
                       cop. 1
   "   "   1890 jD31
                         cop. 2
   "   "   adapted for use of schools jD31r
For treatment of different editions aside from fiction, see 33a.

34 Special classes

X **34a Juvenil books.** Prefix j to call number of books which are specially suitable for young people; e. g.
    Knox. Boy travellers in South America. Q j918
                         qK
    Scudder. Children's book. Q   jqS

34b Large classes. If a class in a library, e. g. poetry, is specially large, it may be wise to use in the book number, an initial and two figures from the tables, instead of one.

34c Local history and genealogy. If a library has many books on local history, the numbers may be given from the name of the place, or in genealogy from the name of the family; e. g.
    Gilman. Story of Boston   974.4
                   B7
    Kimball. Samuel Ames family 929
                   A5
The rule should be uniform in any given library.

34d Books about an author. All books about an author may be placed in a single group with a book number from name of person written about, followd by z; e. g.
    Clarke. Familiar studies in Homer   883
                      H7z
    Nettleship. Essays on Robert Browning's poetry 821
                      B8z

35 Individual biografy

✓ **35a General arrangement.** To keep lives of same person together, assign book numbers from name of person written about and not from author of book.

✝ **35b Length of number.** Use initial of person written about and two figures from tables.
  Add a third figure from tables when necessary to distinguish; e. g.
    Ingram. Elizabeth Barrett Browning 92
                      B88
    Gosse. Robert Browning personalia 92
                      B885

Simplified Book Numbers 57

35c Several lives of same person. Arrange lives of same person alfabeticly by authors, adding author's initial to book number of all after the first; e. g.

Adams.	Christopher Columbus	92 C_72
Elton.	Career of Columbus	92 C_72e
Seelye.	Story of Columbus	j92 C_72s
Winsor.	Christopher Columbus	92 C_72w

When there are many lives of a person, a lower case letter may be added to the number for first book.

35d Authors having same initial. To distinguish authors with same initial, follow analogy of rules for title marks (33b-c); e. g.

Hale.	Life of Washington	92 W_31h
Hayden.	Washington	92 W_31ha
Headley.	Life of Washington	92 W_31he
Henley.	"	92 W_31hn

36 Special schemes

36a Shakspere and other classics. In case of Shakspere, if the library has a large collection, it may be well to adopt a simple special scheme using; e. g.
- x Collected works.
- y Concordances, dictionaries, grammars, etc.
- z Books about the author, biografy, criticism, disputed authorship, etc.

This plan may be followd for other classics; e. g. Homer, Dante, etc. or for any author in case the number of books makes a special arrangement desirable.

The following schemes will guide in assigning book numbers for many books by the same author in the same class.

36b Shakspere scheme. Use S5 followed by lower case initial of plays, arranged alfabeticly, according to 33a-c.

Distinguish two editions of the same play by adding initial of editor or publisher to second edition

In the following scheme, where two or more titles begin with the same letter, two letters are assignd to each, in order that the addition of another letter to distinguish the edition may not separate books which should stand together, e. g. Rolfe's edition of *All's well that ends well* coming in later would be markt S5alr which would place it next another edition of the same play; if the first edition receivd had been markt S5 or S5a the addition of the r for Rolfe would have made the book number S5r or S5ar and have placed the book after *Antony and Cleopatra*.

58   Simplified Library School Rules

Individual works

S5al	All's well that ends well	S5mr	Merry wives of Windsor
S5an	Antony and Cleopatra	S5ms	Midsummer night's dream
S5as	As you like it	S5mu	Much ado about nothing
S5co	Comedy of errors	S5o	Othello
S5cr	Coriolanus	S5pe	Pericles
S5cy	Cymbeline	S5po	Poems, including sonnets
S5h1	Hamlet	S5r2	Richard 2
S5h4	Henry 4	S5r3	Richard 3
S5h5	" 5	S5r4	Romeo and Juliet
S5h6	" 6	S5ta	Taming of the shrew
S5h8	" 8	S5te	Tempest
S5j	Julius Caesar	S5ti	Timon of Athens
S5kj	King John	S5tn	Titus Andronicus
S5kl	King Lear	S5tr	Troilus and Cressida
S5l	Love's labor lost	S5tt	Twelfth night
S5ma	Macbeth	S5tw	Two gentlemen of Verona
S5me	Measure for measure	S5w	Winter's tale
S5mh	Merchant of Venice		

General works

S5x   Collected works
S5y   Concordances, dictionaries, grammar, etc.
S5z   Books about Shakspere, biografy, criticism, disputed authorship, etc.

If a more elaborate scheme is desired, add to S5 the numbers from Shakspere table given in *Library notes*, 2:16.

36c James Fenimore Cooper

C77	Afloat and ashore	C77o	Oak openings
C77a	Autobiography of a pocket-handkerchief	C77p	Pathfinder
		C77pi	Pilot
C77b	Bravo	C77po	Pioneers
C77c	Chainbearer	C77pr	Prairie
C77cr	Crater	C77pu	Precaution
C77d	Deerslayer	C77r	Red rover
C77h	Headsman	C77re	Redskins
C77he	Heidenmauer	C77s	Satanstoe
C77ho	Home as found	C77se	Sea lions
C77hw	Homeward bound	C77sp	Spy
C77j	Jack Tier	C77t	Two admirals
C77l	Last of the Mohicans	C77w	Water-witch
C77li	Lionel Lincoln	C77wa	Ways of the hour
C77m	Mercedes of Castile	C77we	Wept of Wish-ton-wish
C77mi	Miles Wallingford	C77wi	Wing and wing
C77mo	Monikins	C77wy	Wyandotte
C77n	Ned Myers		

36d Sir Walter Scott

S43	Abbot	S43l	Legend of Montrose
S43a	Anne of Geierstein	S43m	Monastery
S43an	Antiquary	S43my	My Aunt Margaret's mirror
S43b	Betrothed	S43o	Old Mortality
S43bl	Black Dwarf	S43p	Peveril of the peak
S43br	Bride of Lammermoor	S43pi	Pirate
S43c	Castle Dangerous	S43q	Quentin Durward
S43ch	Chronicles of the Canongate	S43r	Redgauntlet
S43co	Count Robert of Paris	S43ro	Rob Roy
S43d	Death of the Laird's Jock	S43s	St Ronan's well
S43f	Fair maid of Perth	S43su	Surgeon's daughter
S43fo	Fortunes of Nigel	S43t	Talisman
S43g	Guy Mannering	S43ta	Tapestried chamber
S43h	Heart of Mid-Lothian	S43tw	Two drovers
S43hi	Highland widow	S43w	Waverley
S43i	Ivanhoe	S43wo	Woodstock
S43k	Kenilworth		

37 Arrangement without use of tables

This is recommended only for a small, slowly growing library of less than 1000 volumes, where exact alfabetic order is unimportant.

Under each class keep together names beginning with the same letter by marking books by the first author under any letter with the initial of the author's surname (for exceptions see 34c-d, 35a); books by the second or third author under that letter with the author's initial followd by 1, 2, 3, etc.; e. g. if in class 942, history of England, the first books under G were Green's *History of the English people*, Gardiner's *Outline of English history*, and Guizot's *History of England*, and they were receivd in the order named, the book number of Green's *History* would be G, Gardiner's *Outline* would be G1, and Guizot's *History* G2.

All books, in any class, receivd at one time should be arranged in alfabetic order before the book numbers are assignd; e. g. if G1, G2, G3 are already used and Gardiner, Green and Guizot come in at the same time they should receive the book numbers G4, G5, G6 respectivly.

37a Arbitrary title marks. In fiction or where there are many books by the same author, distinguish different works and different editions, if necessary, by adding to the book number the lower case letters a, b, c, etc.; e. g. if Green's *History of the English people* is G, his *Short history* would be Ga.

> Suggestions for a more accurate arrangement may be found in 33n-d.

For treatment of juvenil books see 34a.

In biografy the book number should be given from the name of the person written about and two or more lives of the same person distinguisht

by adding to the book number the lower case letters a, b, c, etc.; e. g.
if Adams' *Christopher Columbus* is C1, Elton's *Career of Columbus* would
be C1a.

Suggestions for a more accurate arrangement may be found in 35a–d

SIMPLIFIED SHELF LIST RULES

40 Shelf list

Importance. The shelf list is a record of the books in a library in the order in which they stand on the shelves. It is one of three indispensable library records; i. e. the accession book, the card catalog and the shelf list. The accession book is the first of these records to be fild, the shelf list the last. The card catalog is for public use, the accession book and shelf list usually for official use only.

Use

40a Inventory. A library like a business house should, at regular intervals, usually once each year, take an inventory of its stock. Each entry in the shelf list should be compared with the corresponding book on the shelves, all errors corrected and a list of missing books made.

40b Brief clast catalog. As the shelf list is arranged primarily by subjects, it forms a brief clast catalog. This shows in what subjects the library is strong and where additions are needed. It also helps in classifying new books, defining more fully the scope of each class, and showing the kind of books groupt under each subject.

If desired it may be used by the public in connection with a simple author card catalog, or with a dictionary card catalog, in the latter case securing in some measure the advantages of both a dictionary and a clast catalog.

40c Book numbers. Under each class the entries are arranged in the order of the book numbers, and the shelf list shows at a glance what numbers have already been assignd and guards against the use of the same number a second time.

Form

The two forms most commonly used are sheets and cards. For the small library, the list of fiction is best made on cards, all other subjects on sheets. Biografy may also be shelflisted on cards if the rapidity of additions of books in the class makes it desirable. Forms for both a shelf list on sheets and on cards may be found facing p. 67 and on p. 66-67.

For convenience, the rules and sample cards are based on the use of the *Abridged decimal classification* and Cutter's *Alfabetic-order tables altered and fitted with three figures by Kate E. Sanborn.*

40d Sheets. The best form of sheet is 10 x 25 cm (about 4 x 10 inches) and these are fastend into binders, each holding about 100 sheets. Only one subject is written on a sheet so that new sheets can be inserted wherever necessary, the numeric order being maintaind and unnecessary copying avoided.

40e Cards. Some libraries prefer a card shelf list to one on sheets. New entries can be inserted in their exact place and it is consequently never necessary to rewrite. Great care should be taken that cards are not lost or misplaced.

A shelf list on cards is open to the same objection as a card catalog—only one entry can be read at a time, while on the sheets several entries can be read at a glance. The card list is much less safe against removal of entries in case of theft of books and therefore less adapted to an inventory.

41 Shelf list on sheets
General

Rules 41a–r are for a shelf list on 10 x 25 cm sheets. For *variations* necessary for a shelf list on cards see 42a–j.

41a Arrangement of entries. Arrange entries as books are arranged on the shelves; first, by class number, treated decimally; second, by book number, arranged, 1) alfabeticly by the capital letter, 2) numericly by numbers following the capital, treated decimally.

41b Number of entries. Enter only one subject on a sheet, thus allowing for additions, but leave no lines between book entries.

In classes where there are many entries, e. g. individual biografy (41q) it is best to begin each letter on a new sheet, thus avoiding large mixt alfabets and frequent rewriting.

41c Date. Put in the middle of upper margin of recto of each sheet the date when first entry is made; e. g. 13 Je 94, see sample shelf sheet 1-2. When the sheet is withdrawn add after a dash the date of rewriting; e. g. 13 Je 94–17 Ap 98.

41d Class number. Write class number in prominent figures on top line of sheet after the word 'Class'.

41e Book number. Write book number in its column making the figures very clear and distinct.

For use of printed form of letters in call numbers see *Simplified card catalog rules*, 8m.

41f Accession number. Write accession number in its column with dash between inclusive figures; e. g. 3342–7. Give a separate line to all accession numbers not consecutiv; e. g. 2134 v. 1
       2180 v. 2

In case of sets having many accession numbers not consecutiv, the numbers may be arranged in four columns in order to save space. Sample shelf sheet 1.

41g Volume number. Put number of volumes, if more than one, in volume column; if the library contains part of a set, write; e. g. v. 1, or, v. 2–6; write also 2 in 1; 6 in 3; v.9^1, v.9^2. Sample shelf sheet 1–2.

In case of annuals where there is no volume number, use the year in volume column. On bookplates instead of v.1, v.9^1, v.o^1, etc. write 1, 9_1, o_1, etc.

41h Author. Write author's surname in its column, using no punctuation. In case of two joint authors write surname of each; if more than two, write surname of first and '& others.' Sample shelf sheet 1.

In fiction and when necessary to distinguish different authors having same surname, give initials of forenames, using colon abbreviations where applicable.

41i Title. Write brief title in its column with no punctuation. If the shelf list is to be used chiefly as a stock-taking book, use binder's title If used mainly as a subject catalog, use a short or well-known title taking great care in shortening title that it may be at once clear, and comprehensiv. Use library abbreviations in all entries, see 52 Other obvious contractions may also be used if necessary. Add in curves, in briefest form, the name of series if well-known; e. g. (Am. men of let.)

41j Unalfabeted entries. In adding to a shelf list leave one line vacant after the continuous alfabet and add new entries as they come, with no attempt at alfabeting. Whenever a new book number is assignd, pencil it in its proper place in the continuous alfabet; otherwise the whole of the mixt alfabet must be lookt thru to ascertain whether a given book number has been assignd. Rewrite the sheet and combine into one alfabet when the unalfabeted entries become so numerous as to be inconvenient.

41k Old sheets. When the new shelf sheets have been written, arrange withdrawn shelf sheets in order of class numbers and save for reference.

Special cases

41l Second copy. When there is more than one copy of a book, write accession numbers the same as for several volumes (41f) indicating the number of the copy in volume column. If the work has more than one volume, write number of copy in volume column above volume number; e. g.
```
        cop. 2
  3145  v. 1
```

41m Edition. In case of two editions of the same book, add date of each, or number or name of edition, or editor's surname after title. Sample shelf sheet 1. In the classics add editor's surname.

In fiction treat different editions as different copies, unless the edition is considerably alterd or abridged. See *Simplified card catalog rules*, 4h.

41n Special location. When necessary to indicate the location of a book in the reference library or other special collection write or stamp in upper right corner of book number column 'R' or number of room, or other needed designation Sample shelf sheet 1.

41o Changed number. If the class number or any part of it is changed after the book is shelflisted, do not erase entry, but draw a red line thru it, and write in red ink in author column the new class and book number, and enter like a new book in its new place, changing the numbers on book, accession book, and on all catalog entries. If book number alone is changed, draw red line thru it, and write the new number above the old in red ink.

Special classes

41p Serials. In case of periodicals and transactions of societies, etc. still being publisht, put one entry on a sheet and arrange accession numbers in four columns leaving room for missing volumes. Sample shelf sheet 2.

Place an index volume, if unnumberd in the regular series, at the beginning of a set, and mark it with volume number o (zero). If more than one, mark them thus, o^1, o^2, o^3. Above the volume write the years or volumes coverd by the index; e. g. 1840–50 v. o^1, or v. 1–20 v. o^1. Sample shelf sheet 2. See also 41g.

41q Individual biografy. In individual biografy begin each letter on a new sheet, alfabeting by the name of the biografee. Write the word 'Biografee' as the heading of the first half of title column and under this arrange the names of the biografees giving the initials of their forenames. Omit book title unless it is striking. See below.

22 Je 08   Class 92

Book no.	Accession no.	Vol.	Author	Biografee	Title
G76g	4673–4	2	Grant	Grant, U. S.	
G76h	489		Headley	"	Hero boy (Gt. commanders)
G79	1056		Greene, F. V.	Greene, Gen. N.	

41r Genealogy. If the library contains many genealogies of special families, classify them under 929.2 and arrange by the name of the family. Make the entry for genealogy in the same form as for individual biografy, writing the word 'Family' as the heading of the first half of title column instead of the word 'Biografee'. Omit book title except when striking. See below.

23 Je 98   Class 929.2

Book no	Accession no.	Vol.	Author	Family	Title
D3	9023		Ross	De Haven	
D5	76		Morrison	Dinsmore	Irish Among the Scotch-

The name of the author may be omitted when it is the same as the surname of the family written about.

Simplified Shelf List Rules

42 Shelf list on cards

General

The following *variations* from 41a-r are necessary for a shelf list on cards.

42a Size. Use P size cards (7.5 x 12.5 cm). Sample card A.

42b Number of entries. Enter only one work on a card. See also 42e.

42c Class and book number, author and title. In position and indention these entries follow rules for catalog cards, see *Simplified card catalog rules*, 8a-b, m. Sample cards A-E.

42d Accession number. Write accession number on the line below the title close to the first red line. Sample cards A-E.
    When there are many accession numbers not consecutiv, they may be arranged in two columns on the card. Sample card B.

Special cases

42e Second copy. Write the number of the copy after the volume number instead of above it; e. g. 4721   v. 1   cop. 1
                                                                                                  4723   v. 2   "   1
                                                                                                  4722   v. 1   "   2
                                                                                                  4724   v. 2   "   2

See also sample card A.
    The total number of copies may also be penciled below the book number, if desired.

42f Special location. Write or stamp the designation of location in upper right corner of space above the call number. Sample card B.

42g Changed number. Draw a red line thru old number, insert new number in black and change position of the card, or make new card and preserv corrected cards in separate file.

Special classes

42h Serials. If the library has many serials enter them on 10 x 25cm sheets. For form of entry see sample shelf sheet 2.

42i Individual biografy. For arrangement and indention see sample cards C-D. For fulness of entry, see 41q.

42j Genealogy. If genealogy is arranged by the name of the family follow the analogy of individual biografy. Sample card E.

Simplified Library School Rules

Sample cards illustrating shelf list rules

A Form of entries. 42a-d
Second copy. 42c

T36h Thackeray, W: M.
　　　　　Henry Esmond
　　126　　cop. 1
　　843　　cop. 2

B Special location. 42d,f

810^R / qS Stedman & Hutchinson
　　　　　Library Amer. literature
　　53-5　　v. 1-3　　3267　　v 11
　　68-9　　v. 4-5
　　286　　v. 6
　　483　　v. 7
　　709　　v. 8
　　867　　v. 9
　　1045　　v. 10

C Individual biografy. 41q, 42i

92 / R19 　　Randolph, J:
Garland
　　6432-3　　2v.

24 Je 98   Class 810

Book no.	Accession no.	Vol.	Author	Title	
F6	8002		Ford	Literary shop	
G8	217		Griswold	Prose writers of Amer.	1847
G8p	13362		"	"	1870
H3	1743		Hart	Manual of Amer. lit.	
R5	4023-4	2	Richardson	Amer. lit	
R5p	5126		"	Primer of Amer. lit.	
S	53-5	v.1-3	Stedman & Hutchinson	Library of Amer. lit.	v.11
	68-9	v.4-5		483 v.7 867 v.9	3267
	286	v.6		709 v.8 1045 v.10	
T9	2145	2 in 1	Tyler	Hist. of Amer. lit.	

Sample shelf sheet: Serials

Book no.	Accession no.	Vol.	Author	Title		Class 051
A8	612	1857-76 v.0¹	20 Ᵽ 98.	Atlantic monthly 1857-		
	839	1857-88 02				
			91-120 v.1-30	275-6	v.63-64	5124 v.79
			225-8	31-34	837	65	6301 80
					976	66	
			326-9	36-39			
					1277-9	69-71	
					2031	72	
			1204-74	54-61	3196-200	73-77	
			836		624266	78	

Simplified Shelf List Rules

D Individual biografy, distinctive title. 419, 421

92
G76
    Grant, U. S.
  Headley
    Hero boy
489

E Genealogy. 411, 421

929.2
B5
    Bigelow
  Howe
    Report of reunion
1963

[From rules for printing division, University of the State of New York]

CAPITALS, PUNCTUATION, ABBREVIATIONS

50 Capitals

A lavish use of capitals defeats the very purpose for which the letters were distinguished in rank.— GOOLD BROWN

Use lower case exclusivly except for 50a–i.

50a First word. Capitalize first word of every sentence and of every line of poetry.

50b Book titles. Capitalize first word of every title, or alternativ title, of books or periodicals; but not 'laws,' 'acts,' 'statutes,' and similar general terms; e. g., 'provided in laws of 1892, ch. 378.'

This rule allows capitals for Bible, Scriptures, Book of Mormon, etc. Write also Holy Bible, la Sainte Bible, Holy Scriptures of the Old and New testaments.

In quoting book titles omit initial article when not essential to meaning, as it hides the leading word, which should stand out clearly to catch the eye, and treat the word following the article as the first word; e. g. *History of David Grieve* not *The history of David Grieve*. Write also, for example, the *Times*, the *Nation*. See also *Simplified card catalog rules*, 4a, c.

50cc Proper names. Capitalize names of persons, places, and distinctiv but not generic parts of names of political divisions, geografic features (rivers, lakes, mountains, etc.) streets, churches, institutions, organizations, railways, banks, hotels, theaters, halls, business blocks, etc. unless the generic precedes the distinctiv name, or is so far a misnomer as to become distinctiv; e. g. Donaldson's *New Cratylus*, Hudson river, Seneca lake, Plymouth church, Harvard university, Skull and Bones society, Park av., Park avenue hotels (hotels in Park av.) but Park Avenue hotel (distinguishing name of a particular hotel) Hotel Vendome, Lake Michigan, Bracebridge Hall.

50d Proper adjectivs. Capitalize such adjectivs from names of persons or places as reputable usage does not justify in lower case; e. g. American, Italian, but galvanic, boycotted, quixotic, indian (aboriginal American) arabic (in 'arabic figures,' 'gum arabic') etc.

Adjectivs, common nouns, etc. derived from names of persons and places and at first capitalized are constantly losing this distinction as they come into more common use and their origin is forgotten.

50e I and O. Capitalize pronoun I and interjection O.

50f Months, days, etc. Capitalize months, days of week and distinctiv but not generic parts of names of holidays, feast and fast days; e. g. Thanksgiving day, Lincoln's birthday.

50g Epithets. Capitalize epithets:

    a Standing as substitutes for proper names; e. g. the Pretender, the Union, the Empire state;

    b Used as affixes to names of persons, e g. Richard the Lionhearted, Louis le Grand, Friedrich der Grosse.

50h Titles. Capitalize titles immediately prefixt to names of persons or in direct address, e. g. Chancellor Curtis, but chancellor of the University; Secretary Olney, but secretary of state, Mr President, your Honor. But do not capitalize if separated from name by preposition; e. g. earl of Derby, but Earl Spencer; bishop of Albany, but Bishop Doane. Also do not capitalize designations not generally used as titles in direct address; e. g. librarian Smith, instructor Brown, roundsman Rowe. See also 52h.

50i Names of Deity. Capitalize names and titles of the Deity, of Jesus Christ, of the Trinity and of the Virgin Mary, and pronouns referring to God or Christ when used in direct address or whenever the meaning might otherwise be mistaken; e. g. Creator, Almighty, Messiah, Savior, Holy Virgin, *In His name*.

50j Abbreviations. Do not capitalize abbreviations for which reputable usage justifies lower case; e. g. write a.m., p.m., no.

50k Government departments, etc. Do not capitalize government and state departments, legislative bodies, courts, political parties, committees, conventions, conferences, political districts, and public or commercial boards; e. g. U. S. bureau of education, Pennsylvania legislature, bill pending in congress, rules of the court of appeals.

50l Events, etc. Do not capitalize historical events, epochs, documents; e. g. reformation, renaissance, bill of rights, declaration of independence.

50m Race. Do not capitalize gypsy, negro, quadroon, creole, indian meaning an American aborigine; but capitalize Indian meaning a native of India.

51 Punctuation

    There is still much uncertainty and arbitrariness in punctuation, but its chief office is now generally understood to be that of facilitating a clear comprehension of the sense. Close punctuation, characterized especially by the use of many commas, was common in English in the 18th century and is the rule in present French usage; but *open* punctuation, characterized by the avoidance of all pointing not clearly required by the construction, now prevails in the best English usage. In some cases, as in certain legal papers, title-pages, etc. punctuation is wholly omitted.—*Century dictionary*

51a Open punctuation. Follow general rules for punctuation in conformity with the principles of open punctuation. Note particularly the following specified cases.

51b Title-pages. Punctuation on title-pages must sometimes be changed on account of omissions, or to reduce the title to a single sentence, while omitted punctuation necessary to clearness must be supplied. See Cutter, *Rules*, § 207-10.

51c Redundancy. Avoid as far as practicable doubling punctuation marks; i. e. comma and dash, comma and curves, period and comma.

51d Omission of period. Omit period:

1 After Mr, Mrs, Dr, St (meaning Saint; but st. street), Mt, jr, sr, pro tem, viz, vs.

2 After abbreviations in which an apostrofe indicates omitted letters; e. g. sup't, dep't, not sup't., dep't.

3 After marginal references and paragraf numbers.

4 After letters which are used as names but are not abbreviations; e. g. Company A marcht thru K st.; poionaise in A major; the L of a building.

5 After nicknames; e. g. Fred Smith. But distinguish carefully between abbreviations and nicknames; e. g. as an abbreviation for Frederic, write Fred. Smith.

51e Use of period. Use a period before a decimal fraction and between figures denoting hours and minutes; e. g. 86.3, 10.15 p. m.

51f Comma. Distinguish carefully between explanatory or descriptiv, and restrictiv relativ clauses. An explanatory relativ clause must be set off by commas; but a restrictiv clause forming an essential part of its antecedent should not be so separated unless the relativ pronoun refers to each of a series of nouns; e. g. (Explanatory) Sailors, who are generally superstitious, say it is unlucky to embark on Friday. (Restrictiv) The books which help you most are those which make you think most.

Point off numbers of six or more figures with commas, but omit commas in numbers of five figures or less.

When several words are dittoed, use inverted commas under each distinct group of words, not under each word; e. g.

    List of 43 volumes on U. S. history
       "   20   "   "
       "   25   "   economics

not   List of 43 volumes on U. S. history
      "   "   20   "   "   "   "
      "   "   25   "   " economics

51g Apostrofe. Omit apostrofe in plural possessivs of much-used terms when the modifying noun can properly be regarded as an adjectiv; e. g. public libraries act, regents office, regents credentials, etc.

Form the possessiv singular of nouns ending in s, x, or z by adding the apostrofe alone, not 's; e. g. Jones' *Grammar of ornament*, not Jones's.

51h Dash. A dash is sufficient by itself. Do not use with it a comma or other point, except when it follows an abbreviation or a complete sentence.

51i Curves. Use curves to inclose closely connected but unessential matter; i. e. explanatory phrases, translations, definitions.

52 Library abbreviations

On catalog cards use only the abbreviations in 52a, c-h. On other official records, in addition to abbreviations in 52, those given in standard dictionaries may be used, preferring the shortest form consistent with clearness.

Do not add s or double a symbol for plural of abbreviations (except mss for manuscripts); e. g. use p. for page or pages, pt. for part or parts.

52a Colon abbreviations compiled by C: A. Cutter. Use the following abbreviations when only initials would otherwise be used:

A..	Anna	L..	Louisa
A:	Augustus	M:	Mark
B..	Beatrice	M..	Mary
B:	Benjamin	N..	Nancy
C:	Charles	N:	Nicholas
C..	Charlotte	O..	Olivia
D:	David	O:	Otto
D..	Delia	P..	Pauline
E:	Edward	P:	Peter
E..	Elizabeth, Elisabeth	R..	Rebecca
F..	Fanny, Fannie	R:	Richard
F:	Frederick, Frederic	S:	Samuel
G:	George	S..	Sarah
G..	Grace	T..	Theresa
H..	Helen	T:	Thomas
H:	Henry	U:	Ulrich
I:	Isaac	U..	Ursula
I..	Isabella	V:	Victor
J..	Jane	V..	Victoria
J:	John	W..	Wilhelmina
K:	Karl	W:	William
K..	Kate	Z:	Zachary
L:	Lewis	Z..	Zenobia

52b Other name abbreviations. Where great compactness is desired the following name abbreviations may be used in official records not intended for the public.

Semicolons ; and ., are used after the single initial (52a) to indicate the German forms corresponding to the colon abbreviations; e. g. J:

John, J; Johann. Inverted semicolons are used in the same way for the corresponding French form; e. g. J: Jean, J,. Jeanne.

Ab.	Abraham	Gst.	Gustavus, Gustav, Gustave
Alex.	Alexander, Alexandre		
Alf.	Alfred	Hrm.	Herman, Hermann
And.	Andrew, Andreas, André	Hip.	Hippolyte, Hippolytus
Ant.	Anthony, Anton, Antoine	Hu.	Hugh, Hugo, Hugues
Arch.	Archibald, Archambaud	Ign.	Ignatius, Ignaz, Ignace
Art.	Arthur	Jac.	Jacob
A:a.	Augusta	Ja.	James, Jacques
A:in.	Augustin	Jos.	Joseph
A:inus	Augustinus	Jose.	Josephine, Josephe
Bart.	Bartholomew, Bartholomäus, Barthélemi	Jul.	Julius, Jules
		Kath.	Katherine, Katharine
Bern.	Bernard, Bernhard	Lr.	Lawrence, Laurence, Lorenz, Laurent
Cath.	Catherine, Catharine		
Chris.	Christopher, Christoph(f), Christophe	L:e.	Louise
		Marg.	Margaret, Margarethe, Marguerite
Clar.	Clarence		
Dan.	Daniel	Mat.	Matthew, Mathäus, Mathieu
Edg.	Edgar		
Edm.	Edmund, Edmond	Ol.	Oliver, Olivier
Ern.	Ernest, Ernst	Pat.	Patrick
Eug.	Eugene, Eugen	P..a.	Paulina
Fer.	Ferdinand	Ph.	Philip, Philipp, Phillippe
Fitz W:	Fitz William	Rob.	Robert
F..s	Frances	Seb.	Sebastian, Sébastien
Gert.	Gertrude, Gertraud	Ste.	Stephen, Stephan
Gilb.	Gilbert	Thdr.	Theodore, Theodor
Gi. Bat.	Giovanni (Giam) Battista	Tim.	Timothy, Timotheus, Timothée
Greg.	Gregory, Gregor, Grégoire	Wa.	Walter, Walther
		Wash.	Washington
Gu.	Guillaume, Gulielmus		

52c Headings. Use colon abbreviations for English names, also common abbreviations for political, military, professional and honorary titles. For use of titles, see *Simplified card catalog rules*, 3f.

The stard abbreviations may be used at the beginning of a heading. Ordinary abbreviations for states and countries may be used in a heading where they do not stand at the beginning; e. g. Boston (Eng.)

Library Abbreviations

annot.	annotator	*N. Y.	New York
b.	born	*Penn.	Pennsylvania
comnt.	commentator	pseud.	pseudonym
co.	company	pub.	publisher
comp.	compiler	sup't	superintendent
contin.	continuer	tr.	translator
dep't	department	*U. S.	United States
d.	died	&	and (in all languages)
ed.	editor	( )	include name of state or country
*Gt. Br.	Great Britain	?	before a word or figure means
*Mass.	Massachusetts		probably, perhaps *a*

52d Book titles. Never use abbreviations on catalog cards for prominent words in the title. Besides the abbreviations for 'States, titles, etc., (52h) the following may be used in book titles:

Amer. *or* Am.	America, American	geom.	geometry,
apx.	appendix		geometric
biog.	biography,	Ger.	German, Germany
	biographic	hist.	history, historic
chron.	chronology,	hrsg.	herausgegeben
	chronologic	i. e.	id est (that is)
comp.	compiled	incl.	including
cont.	containing	introd.	introduction,
contin.	continued		introductory
cor.	corrected	Ital.	Italian
dep't	department	Lat.	Latin
e. g.	exempli gratia (for	lib.	library
	example)	lit.	literature, literary
ed.	edited, editor,	med.	medical
	edition	misc.	miscellaneous
Eng.	English	ms. mss	manuscript,
enl.	enlarged		manuscripts
fr.	from	nouv.	nouvelle
geog.	geography,	pref.	preface, prefatory
	geographic	pub.	published, publishers
geol.	geology, geologic	rev.	revised

a This practice should be varied when strict adherence to the rule would result in ambiguity. When the first only of two inclusiv dates is in doubt, ? should be writt'n after it, but if the last is the one in doubt, ? should precede it. If both are doubtful ? will preced, et, sm e ? either preceding or following inclusiv numbers might be understood to apply either to both or to one.

Simplified Library School Rules

soc.	society	&	and (in all languages)
sup.	supplement, supplementary, supplementing	&c	et cetera (and so forth)
		–	to and including, or continued
theol.	theology		
tr.	translated, traduit, etc.	...	under misprints
		?	probably, perhaps

52e Imprint and notes. Use size letters given in 52f.
In notes, the abbreviations in all these lists may be used.

asm.	assembly	n. p.	no place
c	copyright; e. g. ^{c} 1882	p.	page
cm	centimeter (about ⅜ in.)	pam.	pamphlet
col.	column	pub.	published
cong.	congress, congressional	pt.	part
doc.	document	rep't	report
ed.	edition	sen.	senate
ex.	executive	ser.	series
f.	folio	sess.	session
facsim.	facsimile	t-p.	title-page
illus.	illustrated, illustrations	v.	volume
leg.	legislature	w.	with
n. d.	no date		

52f Size notation. Use size letter in catalog and other official records; see *Simplified card catalog rules*, 5a, f, g, *Simplified accession rules*, 22b, j.
For all books over 35 cm high the superior figures show in which 10 cm of hight the book falls; e. g. F^2 is between 70 and 80 cm high.

Fold symbol	Size letter			
Never use for size.	*Never use for fold.*			
48°	Fe	outside hight	up to 10	cm
32°	Tt	"	10 " 12.5	"
24°	T	"	12.5 " 15	"
16°	S	"	15 " 17.5	"
12°	D	"	17.5 " 20	"
8°	O	"	20 " 25	"
4°	Q	"	25 " 30	"
f°	F	"	30 " 35	"
	F^1	"	35 " 40	"
	F^2	"	40 " 50	"
	F^3	"	50 " 60	"

A size rule is convenient for measuring books.
For size mark in book numbers see *Simplified book numbers*, 32c.

Library Abbreviations

52g Place of publication. Use the fuller form on catalog cards. In accession book and all other official records use the shorter form. Use the following abbreviations for all languages when the equivalent name contains these letters. Use also the common abbreviations for the states, see 52h.

Alb.	Albany	Lond. *or* L.	London
Bost. *or* B.	Boston	Lpz.	Leipzig
Balt.	Baltimore	N. Y.	New York
Ber.	Berlin	Ox.	Oxford
Camb. *or* Cb.	Cambridge	Par. *or* P.	Paris
Chic. *or* Ch.	Chicago	Phil. *or* Ph.	Philadelphia
Cin.	Cincinnati	San Fran. *or* S. F.	San Francisco
Dub.	Dublin	St L.	St Louis
Edin. *or* Ed.	Edinburgh	U. S.	United States
Eng.	England	Wash. *or* W.	Washington

52h States, titles, etc. All titles which precede the forename of an author in a heading begin with a capital; e. g. Mrs, Capt. Those usually affixt are written with a small letter, e. g. bart., abp.; except letter titles affixt, e. g. D.D., F.R.S. For convenience, this usage has been indicated by capitals and small letters in the following list. For use of titles of honor see *Simplified card catalog rules*, 3f. See also 50h.

A. D.	year of our Lord	C. S. A.	Confederate States of America, Confederate States army
A. R. A.	associate of the royal academy		
abp.	archbishop	C. S. N.	Confederate States navy
Adjt.	adjutant		
adm.	admiral	Cal.	California
Ala.	Alabama	Capt.	captain
Alas.	Alaska	card.	cardinal
Amer. *or* Am.	American	Col.	Colorado, colonel
Ariz.	Arizona	Ct.	Connecticut
Ark.	Arkansas	D. C.	District of Columbia
atty.	attorney	D. C. L.	doctor of civil law
B. A.	British America, bachelor of arts	D. D.	doctor of divinity
		Del.	Delaware
B. C.	before Christ	Eng.	England
bart.	baronet	F. R. S.	fellow of the Royal society
bp.	bishop		

Fla.	Florida	Mrs	mistress
Ga.	Georgia	N. A.	North America
Gen.	general	N. B.	New Brunswick
Gov.	governor	N. C.	North Carolina
Gt. Br.	Great Britain	N. D.	North Dakota
Ia.	Iowa	N. F.	Newfoundland
Id	Idaho	N. H.	New Hampshire
Ill	Illinois	N. J.	New Jersey
Ind.	Indiana	N. M.	New Mexico
Ind. Ter.	Indian Territory	N. S.	Nova Scotia
jr	junior	N. Y.	New York
Kan.	Kansas	Neb.	Nebraska
Ky.	Kentucky	Nev.	Nevada
L. H. D.	doctor of literature	O.	Ohio
L. I.	Long Island	Okl.	Oklahoma
LL. B.	bachelor of laws	Or.	Oregon
LL. D.	doctor of laws	P. E. I.	Prince Edward Island
La.	Louisiana		
Lt.	Lieutenant	Pa.	Pennsylvania
M. A.	master of arts	Ph. D.	doctor of philosophy
M. C.	member of Congress	pres.	president
M. D.	doctor of medicine	R. A.	royal academician
M. P.	member of parliament	R. I.	Rhode Island
		R. N.	royal navy
Maj.	major	Rev.	reverend
marq.	marquis	S. A.	South America
Mass.	Massachusetts	S. C.	South Carolina
Md.	Maryland	S. D.	South Dakota
Me.	Maine	S. T. D.	doctor of sacred theology
Messrs	messieurs (plural of Mr)		
		sr	senior
Mich.	Michigan	St	Saint
Minn.	Minnesota	sup't	superintendent
Miss.	Mississippi	Tenn.	Tennessee
Mlle	mademoiselle	Tex.	Texas
Mme	madame	U. S.	United States
Mo.	Missouri	U. S. A.	United States of America, United States army
Mont.	Montana		
Mr	mister		

U. S. N.	United States navy	W. Va.	West Virginia
Va.	Virginia	Wash.	Washington
visc.	viscount	Wis.	Wisconsin
Vt.	Vermont	Wy.	Wyoming

52i L. B. dates. Use usual abbreviations for days and months on catalog cards. In accession and all purely official records, where compactness is important, use the following, which are the shortest forms that are unmistakable.

Months

Ja F Mr Ap My Je Jl Ag S O N D

Days

Sn M Tu W Th F St

Write; e. g. W 9 S 85 for Wed. Sep. 9th, 1885.

52j Binding. Use the following abbreviations in accession and other purely official records.

bds.	boards	dk.	duck	rus.	russia
cf.	calf	mor.	morocco	sh.	sheep
cl.	cloth, muslin	pap.	paper	vel.	vellum
		ro.	roan		

LIBRARY HANDWRITING

For a fuller discussion see *Library handwriting*, Handbook 11 of the University of the State of New York, 1898, revized from *Library notes*, March 1887. 1: 273-82.

60 Requirements

60a Legibility, speed. Nothing pays better for the time it costs the candidate for a library position than to be able to write a satisfactory library hand. In this, legibility is the main consideration. The catalog hand can not be written as fast as a running business hand, but skilful writers acquire reasonable speed without sacrificing legibility. The time of the writer is, however, of small importance compared with that of the reader.

60b Uniformity. Uniformity is vital to a neat appearance, and has much to do with legibility. Tho every letter is perfectly formd, unless it is uniform with the other letters, the effect is like print in which perfect letters from different fonts are used in the same word.

Uniformity is essential among the various catalogers in the same library, as well as in individual practise. A style should be carefully adopted by a library and all assistants required to follow it.

61 Materials

61a Ink. Use only standard library ink and let it dry without blotting. Ink should flow freely and neither corrode the pen nor mold; it should be permanent and of a uniform color. The New York state library uses Carter's record ink, Stafford's blue writing ink and carmine ink and finds them very satisfactory. Carter's record ink is the standard adopted by Massachusetts for all its recording offices.

61b Inkstands. Good work demands that ink be protected from dust and too free evaporation. The best stand is the 'Perfect' which is of costly construction A good cheap substitute is a bottle with a ground glass stopper and a throat only large enough to allow the pen to reach the ink. The essential requirement is a reservoir of ink shut away from dust, light and air, and feeding easily into a tiny dipping cup for immediate use.

61c Pens. The best work has usually been done with steel pens, but gold fountain pens with short stiff nibs are now made that give equally good results and the fountain is of the greatest practical value. Catalogers uniformly find L. E. Waterman's Ideal fountain pens most satisfactory.

Heath's Volpenna B makes a uniform line and wears well. King's no. 5, no. 9 or some equivalent stub pen gives a heavier, blacker line.

Library Handwriting

Trial will prove which suits the hand best. Fine pens are to be avoided as the lines are trying to weak eyes and on dark days. The ideal library hand should have a clear, strong line which gives maximum legibility.

61d Penholders. Too small holders are apt to cramp the hand in long continued writing. Large hard rubber, wood or cork holders are best. Avoid holders with metal next the fingers

61e Erasers. A good steel eraser kept sharp is essential. Do not remove more of the surface of the paper than necessary. Before attempting to rewrite, rub the erased surface carefully with an ivory paper cutter or some other hard, rounded, polisht surface.

Have a good rubber ink eraser and a brush for removing the crumbs without soiling the paper by brushing off with moist fingers. Circular or obliquely cut bar erasers are best as their sharp edge admits application to a smaller portion of the paper. The ability to erase ink and rewrite on the same surface without leaving a noticeable scar is the best test of the neatness and mechanical skill of a good cataloger.

62 Alfabets

Joind and disjoind hands. Extended experiments indicate that the ideal hand for cataloging is the disjoind. Most persons acquire it more quickly than the connected form and after practise can write it almost as fast, while the result being much more like print is more legible. In fact it is often calld the printing hand. For shelf list, accession books and other official records however, the joind hand may be used, if it can be written much faster. When speed is compared, the printing hand is usually a novelty and the joind the habit of a life time; if constantly used the printing hand is usually found about equal in speed when it has become equally familiar. Librarians should be able to write both hands. Specimens of both alfabets are given on p. 81–82.

63 Brief rules

Joind hand

Rules 63a-i are for joind hand. *Variations* for disjoind hand are given in 63j.

63a Position. Sit squarely at the desk and as nearly erect as possible.

63b Form. Follow the library hand forms of all letters, avoiding any ornament, flourish or lines not essential to the letter.

63c Size. Small letters, taking m as the unit, are one space or 2 millimeters high; i. e. one-third the distance between the rulings of the standard catalog card.

Capitals and extended letters are two spaces high above the base line or run one space below; p, t, &, and figures are one and one half spaces high.

63d Slant. Make letters upright with as little slant as possible, and uniformly the same, preferring a trifle backward rather than forward slant.

63e Spacing. Separate words by space of one m and sentences by two m's. Leave uniform space between letters of a word. Each word should be a unit, and form to the eye a distinct word picture.

63f Shading. Make a uniform black line with no shading. Avoid hair line strokes.

63g Uniformity. Take great pains to have all writing uniform in size, slant, spacing, blackness of lines and forms of letters.

63h Special letters. Dot i and cross t accurately to avoid confusion; e. g. Giulio carelessly dotted has been arranged under Guilio in the catalog. Dot i and j one and one half spaces from line. In foreign languages special care is essential. Avoid slanting r and s differently from other letters. They should be a trifle over one space in hight.

63i Figures. Make the upper part of 3 and 8 a trifle smaller than the lower part. 8 is best made by beginning in the middle.

Disjoind hand

In disjoind hand use the following *variations* from the rules for the joind hand.

63j Special letters. Avoid all unnecessary curves. The principal down strokes in b, d, f, h, i, j, k, l, m, n, p, q, r, t, u and the first line in e should be straight.

Make g and Q in one stroke moving from left to right like the hands of a watch. Begin on the line.

Take special pains with r, as, carelessly made, it is easily mistaken for v or y. Make r and s one space high.

Make the upper part of B, R, S a trifle smaller than the lower part.

Make first and last strokes in M and N vertical, connecting lines oblique.

All strokes in W are obiique.

Specimen alfabets and figures

JOIND HAND

Alternativ forms of D, F, G, H, O, T, V, p will be found in the sample accession and shelf sheets facing p. 52 and 67. Alternativ forms for V, W, Y, f, g, h, k, s, y are given below.

F Alfabets and figures

a B C D D E F G H J g K L
m n O P Q R S T u V v W
W X Y y Z

a b c d e f ß ß s g h h i j k k
l m n o p q r s b t u v w x y y
z

1 2 3 4 5 6 7 8 9 0 &

G Catalog card

973 Parkman, Francis.
P2   Historic handbook of the
     northern tour, Lakes George
     & Champlain, Niagara, Mont
     real, Quebec.   illus. maps, O.
     Bost. 1885.

H Sentences; alternativ forms

Take great pains to have all writing uniform in size, slant, spacing & forms of letters.

Take great pains to have all writing uniform in size, slant, spacing & forms of letters.

DISJOIND HAND

I Alfabet, figures and sentence

A B C D E F G H I J K L M N
O P Q R S T U V W X Y Z
a b c d e f g h i j k l m n o p
q r s t u v w x y z
1 2 3 4 5 6 7 8 9 0 &

Take great pains to have all writing uniform in size, slant, spacing & forms of letters.

BRIEF LIST OF USEFUL BOOKS ON LIBRARY ECONOMY

American library association. Catalog of ' A. L. A.' library, 5000 volumes for a popular library selected by the American library association and shown at the World's Columbian exposition. 592 p. O. Wash. 1893. U. S. Bureau of education, *free*.

—— List of subject headings for use in dictionary catalogs; 2d ed. rev. with an appendix cont. hints on subject cataloging and schemes for subheads under countries and other subjects. 206 p. Q.° Bost. 1898. Library Bureau $2.

—— Papers prepared for the World's library congress held at the Columbian exposition; ed. by Melvil Dewey p. 691-1014, O. Wash. 1896. (U. S.—Education, Bureau of. Publications. no. 224) U. S. Bureau of education, *free*.

Cutter, Charles Ammi. Alfabetic order table, altered and fitted to three figures by K. E. Sanborn. 2v. F. Bost. 1892-95. Library Bureau, v. 1, $1.50; v. 2, $1.

Contents: v. 1, Consonants except S; v. 2, Vowels and S.

—— Expansive classification. Q. Bost. 1891 C: A Cutter, Forbes library, Northampton, Mass *or* Library Bureau, *sheets* $5.

Contents: pt. 1 (complete) First six classifications; pt. 2 (incomplete) Seventh classification.

Prices of separate portions: pt. 1, sheets, $1; Philosophy, Religion, History, Medicine, Local history, bound, $1 each.

—— Rules for a dictionary catalogue. Ed. 3 enl. 140 p. O. Wash. 1891. (U. S.—Education, Bureau of. Public libraries in the U. S. Special report. pt. 2) U. S. Bureau of education, *free*

Denver — Public library. Public library hand-book, Denver; ed by J: C. Dana. 182p illus. S. Denver 1895. Carson-Harper Co. *paper* 35c.; *cloth* 65c.; *mor.* $1.

Dewey, Melvil. Abridged decimal classification and relativ index 192 p. O. Bost. 1895. Library Bureau $1.50.

Also in *Library notes* (subscription price $1) Jan.-Ap. 1896, v. 4 no. 13 14, p.1-192.

—— Decimal classification and relativ index for libraries, clippings, notes, etc. Ed 5. 593 p. O. Bost. 1894 '76 '91 Library Bureau, *sheets* $4; *half turkey or full flex, mor.* $5.

—— New York state library school; library handwriting 21 p. T Alb. 1898. (N. Y. (state)—University. Handbook no. 11) *Single copies free; in quantities, 3c. each*.

Revized from *Library notes*, Mar. 1887, v.1, no. 4. p. 271-72.

—— Library school rules; card catalog rules, accession rules, shelf list rules. Ed. 3 72 p. Q. Bost 1893 Library Bureau, *paper* $1; *cloth* $1.25; *half turkey mor.* $2; *flex. russian mor. with silk* $2.5

—— Simplified Library school rules for popular libraries.   96 p. O.   Bost. 1898.   Library Bureau, *cloth* $1.25.

Contents: Definitions; Card catalog rules; Accession rules; Book numbers; Shelf list rules; Capitals, punctuation, abbreviations; Library handwriting; Brief list of useful books on library economy; Index.
Originally printed in *Library notes* (subscription price $1) Sep. 1898, v.4, no. 16, p. 239-315. Issued separately with some changes and additions.

Library Bureau. Classified illustrated catalog of the library department; a handbook of library fittings and supplies.   146 p. illus. Q. Bost. 1898.   Library Bureau, *free to libraries.*

Library journal; monthly journal of the American library association.   v. 1-5, sq. Q, v. 6-date, sq. O.   N. Y. 1877-date. *Publishers' weekly* office $5 a year.

Library notes; improved methods and labor-savers, June 1886-date.   v. 1-date, O.   Bost. 1887-date.   Library Bureau.
v. 1, cloth $2.50; half turkey mor. $3; v. 2-3 together, cloth $2.50; half turkey mor. $3; v. 4, $1.

Linderfelt, Klas August. Eclectic card catalog rules, author and title entries... with appendix cont. a list of oriental titles of honor and occupations.   104 p. O.   Bost. 1890.   Library Bureau, *paper* $1.25; *cloth* $1.50; *half mor.* $2; *flex. persian mor.* $2.50.

Plummer, Mary Wright. Hints to small libraries.   Ed. 2 rev. & enl.   68 p. illus. O.   N. Y. 1898.   Truslove & Combs 50c.

Public libraries; a monthly review of library matters and methods, 1896-date.   v. 1-date, Q.   Chic. 1896-date.   Library Bureau, Chicago $1 a year.

INDEX

Figures preceded by p. refer to pages, the superior figures indicating the exact place on the page, in ninths; e. g., 11³ means page 11, beginning in the third ninth of the page, i. e. about one third of the way down. Figures followd by letters refer to rules. S. C. refers to sample cards.

Abbreviations, p.11⁴, 52a-j
  in accession book, 22b
  binding, 52j
  colon; definition, p 8²
    on shelf list, 41h
    on subject cards, 3b; S. C. 3, 33
    table, 52a
  dates, 52i
  headings, 52c
  imprint and notes, 52e
  lower case letter, 50j
  name, 3b, 52a-b
  omission of period, 51d
  place of publication, 52g
  on shelf list, 41i
  size symbols, 52f
  states, titles of honor, etc. 52h
  in titles, 52d
' cession, term defind, p 6²
Accession book
  abbreviations, 22b, 52g
  agent noted in, 22p
  author's name, 22h
  binding noted on, 22o
    rebinding noted, 22u
  call number, 22r
    changed, 41o
  cost, record of, 22q
  date; of publication, 22l
    of reception or entry, 22c
  definition, p.6²
  entry; immediate, 22a
    order of, 22a
  form, 20b
  gifts, 22q
  importance, 20a
  imprint, 22j
  invoice book, 22a
  maps, 22v
  paging, 22m
  pamflets, 22g, 22h, 22m
  pictures, 22v
  place of publication, 22k, 52g
  publisher, 22k
  remarks column, 22u
  sample sheet, *facing* p.52
  scientific specimens, 22v
  second copy, 22t
  size record, 22n
    of maps, 22v
  source column, 22p
  statuary, 22v
  title, 22i
  volume number, 22r-s
  what is told by, 20a
Accession clerk, initials, 21a
Accession number, 22d-f
  of added edition, 4h
  assignd to volume not work, 22d
  on back of main autnor card, if, 4h
    22f; S. C. 67
  on bill, 22f
  in book, 22e
  on charts, 22v
  definition, p.6²
  for long sets, 1f
  on maps, 22v
  never reassign, 22d
  on order slip, 22f
  of pamflet volume, 7c
  shelf list, 41f, 42d; S. C. A-E, sample
    sheets *facing* p.66 67
Accession rules, p 47-52
Accession stamp, definition, p.6²
Added edition
  accession number, S. C. 67
  book numbers, 33a
  cataloging, 4h; S. C. 17 19, 19
  definition, p 6²
  on shelf list, 41m; sheet *facing*
    p.66
Added entry, 2w
  arrangement, 11l
  check, 1e
  for clubs, 2j
  for commentator, 2g

cyclopedias, directories and almanacs, 2k
 definition, p 6⁴
 for editor, 2r, 8e
 form of heading, 3c
 fulness of title, 4a
 imprint, 5b; S. C. 2, 6, 29, 31
 for joint authors, 2f; S. C. 31
 for joint editors, commentators, translators, 2f
 for sacred books, 2m
 for societies, 2j
 under title, *see* Title, added entry under
 for translator, 2g, 2r, 8c; S. C. 6
 See also Analytics; Subject entry, added.
Added heading, check, 1c
Added subject number, 11b; S. C. 69
Adjectivs
 capitalization, 50d
 limiting edition, 5c
 numeral, 4f
Affixes
 capitalization, 50g, 52h
 order, 3f
Agent, noted in accession book, 22p
Alfabetic subject catalog, definition, p.6⁴
Alfabetico-clast catalog, definition, p.6⁵
Alfabeting, 9a-h
 by word following article, 4c
 inversion to improve, 3g, 3k
 on shelf list, 41a, 41j
Alfabets, 62
 specimen, p.81⁴, p.82⁷
Almanacs, treatment, 2k
Alternativ title, capitalization, 50b; S.C. 22
Alumni proceedings, 2i
Analytics, 2t, 5k; S. C. 40-41, 43-46, 66, 71
 biografy, S. C. 46
 check, S. C. 39, 42
 definition, p.6⁵
 indention, 8f
 subject analytic, 7b; S C. 44-45, 66, 71
 title, 5k; S C. 41
Analyze, term defind, p.6⁶
Annuals without volume number on shelf list, 41g
Anonymous book, 2e; S. C. 15-16
 on accession book, 22h
 author found, S. C. 17-19
 definition, p.6⁷
Anonymous classics, 2m; S. C. 56
 list, 2m
Apostrofe, use of, 51g

Appendix, analytic for, 5k
Arabian nights entertainments, 2m; S. C. 56
Arabic, capitalization, 50d
Arabic figures
 on accession book, 22l
 in book titles, 4f; S. C. 15, 49, 63
 for rulers, popes, etc. 2q
Arrangement
 of books in each class, 30
 of cards in clast catalog; 11k
 in name catalog, 11l
 of names, 9a-h
 of shelf list entries, 41a, 41j
Article, initial
 in foreign languages, 4c; S. C. 62
 omission from title, 2c, 4a, 50b
 in quoted titles, 50b
 when retaind, 4c
Atlas, 5g; S. C. 50
Author analytic, S. C. 40, 43
 check, S. C. 42
Author bibliografy, 11f
Author card
 accession number, 1f
 checks on, 1c-f
 definition, p.6⁷
 no reference number on, 11b
Author catalog
 definition, p.6⁸
Author entry
 authors of separate works publisht together, 2f
 check, 1a
 definition, p.6⁹
 form of heading, 3a
 main entry, 2a; S. C. 1, 5, 32, 63 6²
 See also Joint authors.
Author's name
 on accession book, 22h
 indention, 8a
 not in v. 1, 2c
 on shelf list, 41h, 42c; S. C. A; sheet *facing* p.66
 in title, 4d
 on added title card, S. C. 2
 on translator card, S. C. 6
 See also Biografy; Criticism; Forenames; Genealogy; Heading, form of; Surnames.
Autobiografy, treatment, 11d; S. C. 74

Banks, capitalization, 50c
Bastard title, definition, p.8⁹
Bible, 2l, 11c; S. C. 62, 72-73
 capitalization, 50b

Index

Bibliografee, definition, p.6*
Bibliografy
   arrangement in catalog, 11l
   author, 11f
   blue cards for, 12
   definition, p.7^1
   word 'see' in black, 12
Bibliografy of library economy, p. 83-84
Bill
   accession number on, 22f
   compared and verified, 21a
Binder's title
   definition, p.7^2
   entry for, 2s
   on shelf list, 41i
Bindings
   abbreviations, 52j
   materials noted on accession book, 22o
   rebinding noted on accession book, 22u
Biografee
   definition, p.7^3
   name in red, 11d
Biografy
   analytic, S. C. 46
   arrangement of cards, 11l
   book numbers, 35a-d
   in clast catalog, 11d; S. C. 33
   collectiv, 11d
   green cards for, 12
   main author entry, S. C. 32
   in name catalog, 11e; S. C. 33
   on shelf list, 41b, 41q, 42i; S. C. C-D
   shelf list on cards, 40c
   of special classes, 11d
   word 'see' in black, 12
Blue cards for bibliografy, 12
Blue ink, 8m, 61a
Body, responsible, entry under, 2d
Book card, definition, p.7^5
Book numbers, 30-37
   on accession book, 22r
   added editions, 33a
   alfabetic order, 31a
   arrangement without table, 37
   author arrangement, 32a
   books about an author, 34d
   biografy; authors having same initial, 35d
   individual, 35a-d
   length of number, 35b
   several lives, 35c
   changed, 41o
   Cutter tables, 32a

   definition, p.7^5
   form, 31e
   genealogy, 34c
   juvenil books, 31a
   large books, 32e
   large classes, 31b
   length of number, 32c-d
   local history, 34c
   position, 8m
   principles, 31b
   purpose, 31a
   second copy, 33d
   on series card, 2u; S. C. 31, 36
   shelf list, 41e, 42c; S. C. A-E; sheets *facing* p 66-67
   special schemes, 36a-d
   title marks, 33a-c
      arbitrary, 37
Book-plate
   call number on, 31a
   definition, p.7^4
   position, 23b
Book pocket, definition, p.7^4
Bracket, definition, p.7^6
Broadside
   definition, p.7^5
   size record, 5h
Bureaus, 3g
Business blocks, capitalization, 50c

Call number
   on accession book, 22r
   of added edition, S. C. 17
   on back of book, 31a
   on bookplate, 31a
   definition, p.7^6
   on extra card, 8j; S. C. 34
   of index, S. C. 40
   ink, 8m
   with volume number included, 8m; S. C 46, 49
Canary cards for criticism, 12; S. C. 77-78
Canonized persons, 2q
Capitals general rules, 50a-m
   size, 63c
Cards, catalog
   abbreviations used on, 52
   size, p.29^1, 42a
Cards, shelf list, 40e, S. C. A-E
   author's name, 42c
   position of book number, 42c
   position of class number, 42c
   size, 42a
   title, 42c
Carter's record ink, 61

88   Simplified Library School Rules

Catalog
    alfabetic subject, p.6[4]
    alfabetico-clast, p.6[8]
    author, p 6[n]
    clast, p 7[9]-8[1]
    definition, p.7[7]
    dictionary, p.8[1]
    name, p.9[6]
    subject, p.10[9]
Cataloger, check, 1b
Catalogs, treatment, 2h; S. C. 54
Change of name
    of periodical; 2j. S. C. 47 48
       check for added entry, S. C. 47
    of persons, 2n
Charts, accession number, 22v
Checks
    in books, 1a-b
    on cards, 1c-f
    for completed work only, p.11[7]
    definition, p.7[8]
Churches, capitalization, 50c
Cities
    arrangement in catalog, 9g
    entry under, 2d
    form of heading, 3h
    dash, 3j
    names in English, 3h
    reference from, S. C. 55
Class number
    on accession book, 22r
    for added subject card, 11b; S. C. 45-46, 69-71
    arrangement by, 11k
    changed, 41o, 42g
    definition, p.7[9]
    position on catalog cards, 8m
    on series cards, 2u; S. C. 34, 36
    on shelf list, 41d,42c: S.C. B-E; sheets *facing* p.66-67
Classics
    book numbers, 36a
    editor's name on shelf list, 41m
    list of anonymous, 2m
    treatment of anonymous, 2m; S. C. 56
Clast catalog
    definition, p 7[9]-8[1]
    general rules, 11a-l
Clubs, periodicals publisht by, 2j
Collate, term defind, p.8[1]
Collections, 2a
    accession number for each volume, 22d
Collectiv biografy, 11d
College societies, 2i

Colon abbreviations, 52a
    on accession book, 22b
    definition, p.8[a]
    on shelf list, 41h
    on subject cards, 3b; S. C. 3, 33
Colord cards, 12
Comma, use of, 51f
Commentaries, treatment, 2g
    See also Joint editors, commentators, translators.
Commercial boards, capitalization, 50k
Compiler, entry under, 2a
Compound names, entry, 3e; S C. 8
Contents, 6a; S. C. 5
    indention, 8i
Continuations, 2j, 5c; S. C. 47
    accession number for each volume, 22d
    definition, p.8[a]
    See also Periodicals.
Contractions, on shelf list, 41i
Conventions, capitalization, 50k
Cooper, J. F., book numbers, 36c
Copyright date
    on accession book, 22l
    on cards, 5j; S. C. 20, 47
Cost
    in accession book, 22q
    in book, 21c
    on order slip, 21b
    of rebinding, 22u
Countries
    arrangement in catalog, 9g
    entry under, 2d, 3g; S. C. 51-52
    English form of name, 3h
    heading, dash in, 3j; S. C. 51-52
Courts, capitalization, 50k
Criticism
    arrangement in catalog, 11l
    canary cards for, 12
    general, 11g; S. C. 75-76
    of individual work, 11h; S. C. 77-78
    word 'see' in black, 12
Cross reference, *see* Reference.
Curves
    in analytics, 5k
    definition, p.8[a]
    inclosing initial article, 4c
    inclosing series note, 2u
    use, 51i
Cutter tables
    book numbers, 32a
    colon abbreviations, 52a
Cyclopedias, 2k; S. C. 49
    indention, 8c

Index 89

Dash
  for added edition, 4h; S. C. 17-19, 49
  in heading, 3j; S. C. 50-52
  as punctuation, 51h

Dates
  on accession book; copyright, 22l
  of publication, 22l
  of entry or reception, 22c
  of added edition, 4h
  of birth and death; used to distinguish, 3f
  distance from name, 8k
  copyright 5j; S. C. 20, 47
  in imprint, 5a; S C, 1-3
  inclusiv, 5j, 6b; S. C. 20, 47, 49
  of preface, 5j
  of publication; approximate, 5j
  unknown, 5j; S. C. 21
  varying, 5j; S. C 49
  of receipt; in book, 21c
  on order slip, 21b
  on shelf list, 41c; sheets *facing* p.66-67

Dates, L. B.
  abbreviations, 52i
  definition, p 9⁴

Days of week, abbreviations, 52i

Debates, parties in, 2f

Definitions, p 6-11

Dictionary catalog
  definition, p.8⁴
  general rules, 10a-d

Directories, 2k

Disjoind hand, 62, 63j
  specimen alfabets and figures, p 82⁷

Ditto marks
  on accession book, 22d
  use of, 51f

Documents, capitalization, 50l
  See also Government departments.

Duplicate
  definition, p.8⁶
  withdrawal noted on accession book, 22u
  See also Fiction; Second copy

Ecclesiastical dignitaries, entry, 2p

Edition, 5c; S. C. 30, 49
  definition, p.8⁵
  different editions in set, 5c
  distinguisht by note, S C. 42
  language for; in imprint, 5c
  in title, 5c
  place in imprint, 5a; S. C. 17, 51, 55
  on shelf list, 41m; sheets *facing* p 66-67

  title references for different editions, 2s
  See also Added edition

Editor
  arrangement of cards, 11l
  entry in place of author analytic, 2t
  name in title, 1b; S. C. 56-55
  reference to series, 2u; S. C. 35
  on shelf list, 41m
  added entry under; 2r
  for cyclopedias, directories, almanacs, 2k
  check, 1c
  indention, 8c
  form of name, 3c
  for sacred books, 2m
  main entry under; 2n; S. C 20
  for Bible, 11c
  for series, 2u
  See also Joint editors, commentators, translators.

Embossing stamp, use of, 23a

English language
  for edition in imprint, 5c
  for identification of place, 5i
  for names of cities, 3h
  compound names, 3c
  for name of country, 3g
  names with prefix, 3d
  for notes, 6b

Entries on back of card, 1e f; S. C. 6;
  accession number, 1f, 22f; S C. 6;
  for extra cards, 2u
  for pamflets, 7c
  for subject analytics, 2t
  subject headings, 10d; S. C. 67

Entry, definition, p. 8⁴

Epithets, capitalization, 50g

Epochs, capitalization, 50l

Erasers, 61e

Exchanges, noted on accession book, 22u

Extra card, 8j; S. C. 34, 47
  identification, 2u

Family name
  for genealogy, 11i; S C. 70
  reference from, 20; S C. -

Fasts and feasts, capitalization, 50l

Fiction
  arbitrary title marks, 37
  author on shelf list 41h
  book number for 2d copy, 31d
  class number, 30
  duplicates, 4j
  minor differences, 4h
  on shelf list, 41m

single title card for, 2s
shelf list on cards, 4oc
title cards for, 2s
Figures, arabic
on accession book, 22l
in book titles, 4f; S. C. 15, 49, 63
in headings, 3a
for rulers, popes, etc. 2q
rules for writing, 63c, 63i
specimen, p.81⁶, p.82ʰ
First name, see Forename.
First word, entry under, 2e
Fixt location, definition, p.8⁷
Fold symbol, definition, p.8⁸
Forenames
 abbreviations, 52a
 on added entry cards, 3c
 arrangement in catalog, 9d
 on author cards, 3a; S. C. 30-31
 on biografy card, S. C. 33
 of joint authors, 2f
 persons enterd under, 2q; S. C. 38
 on reference cards, 3c
 on subject cards, 3b; S. C. 3-4, 33
Fountain pens, 61c
Fraternities, 2i
French names with prefix, 3d
Friars, entry, 2q

Genealogy, 11i; S. C. 79
book numbers, 34c
on shelf list, 41r, 42j; S. C. E
Geografic features, capitalization, 50c
German names with prefix, 3d; S. C. 10-12
Gifts, on accession book, 22q
Government departments
 capitalization, 50k
 heading, form of, 3g; S. C. 50-51
  dash in, 3j
 publications not anonymous, p.67
 reference from, S. C. 52
Greek names, 3a
Green cards for biografy, 12
Guide card
 definition, p. 8ᵏ
 with information about author, 3f

Half-binding
 definition, p. 8ᵃ
 on accession book, 22o
Half-title
 definition, p. 8ᵇ
 entry, 2s
Handwriting, 60-63
 specimen alfabets and figures, p.81-82

Heading
 abbreviations used in, 52c
 definition, p.9¹
 form of; general rules, 3a-k
  in biografy, 11d; S. C. 33, 46
 represented by dash for added edition, 4h
 spacing, 8k
Heath's pens, 61c
Historical events, capitalization, 50l
History, local, 11j; S. C. 80
 book numbers, 34c
Holidays, capitalization, 50f
Hotels, capitalization, 50c
Hyphen names
 entry, 3e
 reference, S. C. 8

Illustrations, place in imprint, 5a; S. C. 1, 20, 49
Imperfections, notes on cards, 5d, 6b; S. C. 53
Imprint, 5a-k
 abbreviations, 52c
 on accession book, 22j
 of added edition, 4h; S. C. 17-19, 49
 of analytic with independent title-page, 5k; S. C. 44
 arrangement, 5a; S. C. 1
 atlas, work with, S. C. 50
 of continuations, 5e; S. C. 47
 definition, p. 9²
 edition, place in, S. C. 51, 58
 fulness, 5b
 on main cards, 11a
 map, S. C. 57
 spacing, 8l
Incomplete work, treatment, 5d
Indention, 8a-j
 added entry for editor, translator, etc. 8e
 analytics, 8f; S. C. 40-41, 43-46
 author's name, 8a
 contents, 8i
 cyclopedia, 8c; S. C. 49
 definition, p.9³
 name references, 8g; S. C. 7-13
 notes, 6b, 8h; S. C. 21, 53, 79
 periodicals, 8c; S. C. 47-48
 'see' and 'see also,' references, 8g; S. C. 59-61
 series, 8i
 subject heading, 8d; S. C. 3, 19, 64-66
 title, 8b, 8e S. C. 1-4, 15, 56
Independent books, bound together, 7c
Independent title-page, 5k; S. C. 44-45

Index

Index volumes, 1h; S. C. 1)
  on shelf list, 41p
Indian, capitalization, 50d, 50m
Individual entry, definition, p. 9⁵
Initial article, *see* Article, initial.
Initials
  of accession clerk, 21a
  arrangement in catalog, od ·
  of cataloger, 1b
  check for entry, 1d, S. C. 22
  entry under, 2b; S. C. 21
  last initial first, 2b
  reference from, 2b, 2n; S. C. 23-24
  term defined, p.9¹
  See also Forenames.
Ink, 61a
Inkstands, 61b
Institutions
  capitalization, 50c
  entry under; 2d; S. C. 54
  dash in heading, 3j
  form of heading, 3i
  references for, 3i; S. C. 55
Inversion in heading, 3k; S. C. 51-52

Joind hand, 62, 63a-i
  specimen alfabets and figures, p.81²
Joint authors
  on accession book, 22h
  check, S C. 30
  entry, 2f; S. C. 30-31, S. C. 57
  place in catalog, 11l
  on shelf list, 41h
Joint editors, commentators, translators, added entries, 2f
Juvenil books, book numbers, 34a

Keys, treatment, 4h
Kings, form of heading, S. C. 35
King's pens, 61c
Koran, treatment, 2m

L. B. dates, 52i
  definition, p.9¹
Lakes, capitalization, 50c
Language
  of book, note stating, 6b
  for edition, 5e
  for hereditary titles, 3a
  See also English language ; French names
Latin names, 3a
Legislativ bodies, capitalization, 50k
Letters
  in call numbers, 8m
  forms, 63b
  shading, 63f

size, 63e
slant, 63d
special, 63h, 63j
uniformity, 63g
Library abbreviations, 52a-
Library catalogs, entry, 2h, 3b-i, S C 54, 55
Library economy, brief bibliografy, p 53-81
Library handwriting, 60-63
  specimen alfabets and figures, p. 81-82
Local history, 11j; S. C. 50
  book numbers, 34c
Losses noted on accession book, 22n
Lower-case letter, definition, p. 9⁵

Main entry
  accession number on, 1f, 4b, 22f, S. C. 67
  author, 2a; S. C. 1, 5
  check, 1a
  definition, p 9⁵
  general rules, 2a-q
  of independent books bound together, 7c
  subject, 7a; S. C. 3-4, 16, 19, 33, 64, 66
Manuscripts, abbreviation for, 52
Maps
  on accession book, 22v
  accession number on, 22v
  record on cards, 5a; S. C. 20, 40
  size record, 5h; S. C. 57
  stamp of ownership, 23a
Married women, entry, 2o
Misprints on title-page, 4e; S. C. 41
Months, abbreviations, 52i
Mottoes, omit from title-page, 2e, 4a
Mountains, capitalization, 50c
Municipal department, form of heading, 3h

Name abbreviations
  colon, 52a
  other, 52b
Name catalog, definition, p.9⁴
Name references, 8g, S. C. 5, 7 11, 21 21 26, 28
  definition, p.9⁴
  form of author's name, 3e
Names
  arrangement in catalog, 9a-h
  author's repeated in title, 4d
  of cities, 3b
  of countries, English form for, 3g
  English and foreign with prefix, 3d, S. C. 10-12

Greek, 3a
Latin, 3a
of persons, change of, 2n
of societies, spelling, 3i
spelling in notes, 3a
  See also Biografy; Criticism; Forenames; Genealogy; Heading, form of; Surnames, and *special classes of persons.*
New edition, place on card, S. C. 58
Newspapers, capitalization of names, 50b
Noblemen, entry, 20; S. C. 7
Notes
  abbreviations, 52e
  in accession book, 22u
  general rules, 6b
  indention, 6b, 8h; S. C. 53, 79
  missing volumes, 5d; S. C. 53
  no more publisht, 5d; S. C. 53
  for pamflets, 7c
  periodicals, S. C. 47
  series, definition, p. 10⁸
  spelling of names, 3a
  on subject cards, 4a, 5c
Novels, *see* Fiction.
Numbering stamp, *see* Accession stamp.
Numbers
  pointing off, 51f
  in title, 4f; S. C. 15, 56, 63
  See also Accession number; Added subject number; Call number; Figures; Series number.
Numeral adjectivs, 4f

Official bodies, 3g-k; S. C. 51-52
Omissions from title page, 2e, 4a; S. C. 58
Order checks, 21a-d
Order index, definition, p. 9⁷
Order slip
  accession number, 22f
  definition, p 9⁷
  on reception of book, 21b
Organizations, capitalization, 50c
Oriental writers, 2q

Pages, abbreviation for, 52
Paging, on accession book, 22m
Pamflets, 7c
  on accession book, 22g
  author entry on accession book, 22h
  paging on accession book, 22m
Parentheses, *see* Curves.
Partial title, added entry for, 2k; S. C. 29
Parts, abbreviation for, 52
Pencil entries, 5d, p 29³; S. C. 47, 53
  on title-page, 1a, 2c
Penholders, 61d
Pens, 61c

Period
  when omitted, 51d
  use, 51e
Periodicals, 2j; S. C. 47-48
  accession number on each volume, 22d
  change of name, 2j; S C. 47-48
  check for added entry, S. C. 47
  indention, 8c
  on shelf list, 41p, 42b; sheet *facing* p 67
  volume record, 5e
Person, place, title, arrangement in catalog, 9c
Pictures on accession book, 22v
Place of publication
  abbreviations, 52g
  on accession book, 22k
  in language of title-page, 5i
  more than one, 5i
  position in imprint, 5a; S. C. 1, 49
  unknown, 5i; S. C. 21
Places, names of
  arrangement, 9c
  capitalization, 50c
  See also Cities; Countries.
Plates
  stamping, 23a
  volume of, 5g
Plays, title cards for, 2s
Pocketing, 23c
Poems, title cards for, 2s
Political divisions, capitalization, 50c
Political parties, capitalization, 50k
Popes
  arabic numerals for, 2q
  English form of title, 3a
  entry 2p, 2q
Portraits, stamping, 23a
Preface, analytic for, 5k; S. C. 46
Preface date, 5j
Prefixt titles, 52h
Prefixes
  arrangement in catalog, 9e
  English and foreign names, 3d
  name reference, S. C. 11-12
Printing hand, 62, 63j
  specimen alfabets and figures, p 82⁷
Private mark in book, 21d
Proceedings, 2i, 2j
Pseudonym, definition, p. 9⁸
Pseudonymous books, 2c; S. C. 25-29
  check for reference, 1d; S. C. 25
  main entry under pseudonym, 2c; S. C. 27

Index

references, 2c; S C 26 18
Public libraries, publications of, 2h, ih 1,
    S. C. 54
Publication, date of, *see* Dates of publication.
Publication, place of, *see* Place of publication.
Publisher
    on accession book, 22k
    added entry for, 2k
Punctuation, rules, 51a-i

Railways, capitalization, 50c
Rare books, titles, 4g
Rebinding, note on accession book, 22u
Receipt index
    definition, p.9⁸
    filed alfabeticly, 21b
Recto, definition, p.9⁸
Red ink, 61a
    for family name, 11i
    local history heading, 11j
    name of biografee, 11d
    name of person criticized, 11g
    number of copies, p 29³
    subject headings, p. 29³, 10A
    subject numbers, p 29³, 8m, 11b
    title of criticized work, 11h
Reference books, location marks, 41n, 42f
References
    for Bible, 11c; S. C. 73
    no call number, 8m
    from changed names, 2n
    checks, 1d
    classes requiring, 2v-w
    from college, 2i
    compound names; 3e; S. C. 8
    definition, p.9⁹
    from editor to series, S. C. 35
    from family name of nobleman, 2o,
        S. C. 7
    form of heading, 3c
    from government department, S.C.52
    indention, 8g; S. C 7-14, 24, 26, 48,
        59-61
    from initials, 2b, 2n; S. C. 22-23
    for married women, 2n
    from name of editor, 2u
    name references, S. C. 7-14
    from place, 3i
    from prefix, 3d; S. C. 11-12
    to real name, 2c; S. C. 26
    from real name to pseudonym, 2c,
        S. C. 28

'see,' sg, 10a; S. C. 21 24, 26, 28,
    48, 59
'see also,' sg, 10a, S. C. 52 60 61
    for societies and institutions, 3
    from societies, 2i
    from title of book, 2s, S. C. 14
    from title of ecclesiastical dignitary,
        2p
    from title of nobleman, 2o
    from title of series, 2u; S. C. 37
    See also Subject references
Relativ location, definition, p 9⁹-10¹
Remarks column in accession book, 22r
Residence, used to distinguish, 3f
Rivers, capitalization, 50c
Roman numerals, never use, 4f
Rulers, 2q
    arabic numerals for, 2q
    English form of title, 3a, S. C. 38
Running title
    definition, p.10¹
    entry for, 2s

Sacred books, 2m
    capitalization, 50b
Sacred persons, capitalization, 50i
Saints, 2q
Sales, noted on accession book, 22u
Samples
    accession sheet, *facing* p.52
    catalog cards, p.29-30
    shelf list cards, p.66-67
    shelf sheets, *facing* p 66-67
Scientific specimens on accession book,
    22v
Scott, Sir Walter, book numbers, 36d
Second copy, 4i; S. C. 63-71
    on accession book, 22t
    book numbers, 33d
    on shelf list, 41l, 42e; S. C. A
Secondary entry, *see* Added entry.
'See' reference, sg, 10a, S C 7 13 21
    24, 26, 28, 35, 37, 48, 59
'See also' reference, sg, 10a; S. C. 52,
    60-61
Serial, definition, p.10²
    See also Periodicals.
Series, 2u; S. C. 34 37
    accession number for each volume,
        22d
    check for added entry, 1c, S. C. 32
    check for reference, 1d, S. C. 36
    indention, 81
    never precedes title, 2e
    spacing of card, 2u, S. C. 34, 36
Series entry, definition, p 10²

Series note, 2n. 4a; S. C. 32-33
  definition, p 10³
  for edition, 5c
  on shelf list, 41i
Series number, 2u, 4a; S. C. 38
  disregard as first word, 2e
  place on card, 8i; S. C. 36
Sets
  in accession book, 22d
  accession numbers; if, 22f
    on shelf list, 41f
  cost record on accession book, 22q
  containing different editions, 5c
  missing volumes, 5d; S. C. 53
  volume number in call number for part, 8m; S. C. 46, 49
  volumes of varying size, 5f
Shakspere, book numbers, 36a-b
Shelf list, p.61-67
  abbreviations, 41i
  accession number, 41f, 42d; S. C. A-E, sheets *facing* p.66-67
  annuals without volume number, 41g
  arrangement of entries, 41a
  author's name, 41h, 42c; S. C. A-E, sheets *facing* p.66-67
    on shelf list card, 42c
  biografy, individual, 41b, 41q, 42i; S. C. C-D
  book number, 41e, 42c; S. C. A-E, sheets *facing* p.66-67
    position, 42c
  changed number, 41o, 42g
  class number; 41d, 42c; S. C. B-E, sheets *facing* p.66-67
    position, 42c
  as class catalog, 40b
  contractions, 41i
  date, 41c
  definition, p.10⁴
  edition, 41m, sheets *facing* p.66-67
  editors, 41m
  fiction duplicates, 41m
  form, 40c-e
  genealogy, 41r, 42j; S. C. E
  importance, 40
  index volume, 41p
  as inventory, 40a
  number of entries; on card, 42b
    on sheet, 41b
  rewritten, 41j-k
  second copy, 41l, 42c; S. C. A
  serials, 41p, 42h, sheet *facing* p. 67
  series, 41i
  size of cards, 42a

special location marks, 41n, 42f; S. C. B, sheets *facing* p 66-67
  title, 41i. 42c; S. C. A-E, sheets *facing* p 66-67
  on shelf list card, 42c
  unalfabeted entries, 41j
  use in assigning book numbers, 40c
  volume numbers, 41g; S. C. B, sheets *facing* p 66-67
  withdrawn sheets, 41k
Shelf number
  definition, p 10⁵
  for fiction, 30
  See also Book numbers ; Call numbers.
Signature, definition, p 10⁵
Size
  on accession book, 22n
  of atlas, 5g
  of cards, p 29ᵃ, 42a
  of letters and figures, 63c
  of maps, 5h; S C. 57
  record on accession book, 22v
  place in imprint, 5a; S. C. 1, 17
  variations in sets, 5f; S. C. 50
Size letters, 52f
  definition, p.10ᵃ
Size mark
  in book numbers, 32e
  definition, p 10⁷
Size notation, 52f
Size rule, definition, p.10⁷
Sobriquets, 3f
Societies
  college, 2i
  entry under; 2d, 2j; S. C. 53
  form of heading, 3i
  periodicals publisht by, 2j
  publications not auonymous p.67
  references for, 31
Source, record in book, 21c
Source column in accession book, 22p
Sovereigns
  arabic numerals for, 2q
  English form of title, 3a; S. C. 38
  entry, 2p, 2q
Spacing, 8 k-l, 63e; S. C. 1, 6-7, 12, 30
Special author numbers, 36a-d
Spelling
  of names; in headings, 3a
    in notes, 3a
  of societies, 3i
  peculiarities. 4c; S. C. 36, 38, 44
  reference from different forms, S. C. 13
  See also English language.

Index

Stafford's inks, 61a
Stamp, *see* Embossing stamp.
Stamping, 23a
Standard sizes, definition, p. 10*
State, entry under, 3g
State departments, capitalization, 50k
States
 abbreviations, 52h
 distinguisht from city, 2d
 name added, 2d; S. C. 55
Statuary, on accession book, 22v
Streets, capitalization, 50c
Striking titles, 2s ¹
Sub-title, *see* Alternativ title.
Subject card, definition, p. 10*
Subject catalog
 definition, p. 10*
 alfabetic subject catalog, p. 6¹
Subject entry, 7a-c
 added, 7a; S. C. 65, 70
 analytics noted on back of author
  card, 2t
 author's name, 3b; S. C. 33, 64
 autobiografy, S. C. 74
 biografic analytic, S. C. 46
 class numbers, 11a
 definition, p. 10*
 fulness of title, 4a
 for independents, 7c
 main entry,7a; S.C 3-4. 10,10,33,64,69
 pamflets, 7c
 subject analytics; 2t, 7b, 11b
  clast catalog, S. C. 45, 71
  dictionary catalog. S C. 44, 46, 66
 subordinate headings, 11a
Subject heading, S. C. 16, 33, 62
 biografy,S. C. 33
 criticism, S. C. 75-78
 definition, p.11¹
 in dictionary catalog, 10a
 genealogy, S. C 79
 indention, 8d; S. C. 3, 64-66
 local history, S. C. 80
 record on cards, 10d; S. C. 67
Subject numbers in red, 8n
 omit from biografee cards in name
  catalog, 11c
Subject references, 7a, 11b; S C. 65, 70
 definition, p 11¹
 dictionary catalog, S. C 59-61
Supplements, treatment, 4h, S. C. 11
Surnames
 arrangement in catalog, 6d
 entry under, 2a
 on subject cards, 3b

Talmud, treatment, 2m
Thanksgiving day, capitalization, 5f
Theaters, capitalization, 50s
Title, 4a-i
 abbreviations in, 52d
 on accession book, 22i
 of added edition, 4h
 added entry under, 2s, S. C. 2
  added edition, S. C. 15
  when author of anonym is found
   2e; S. C. 18
  check, 1c; S. C. 1, 5, 17, 27
  for cyclopedias, directories and
   almanacs, 2k
  duplicates in fiction, 2s
  for book enterd under initials, 2b
  fulness, 4a
  indention, 8e
  for novels, plays, striking titles,
   etc. 2s
  for partial title, 2k; S. C. 20
  for pseudonymous books, 2c
  for society publications, 2j
  title analytic, S. C. 41
  check, S. C. 30
 alternativ, capitalization, 50b; S. C.
  22
 in analytics, 5k; S. C. 40-41, 43-46, 66
 author's name in, 4d
 binder's; on shelf list, 41i
  definition, p.7*
 of criticized work, 11h; S. C. 77-78
 definition, p.11*
 edition in, 5c
 editor's name in, 4b; S. C. 50-55
 first word, 2e, 50b
 fulness on author card ; clast catalog,
  S. C. 68
 dictionary catalog, S. C. 63
 fulness on subject card, clast catalog,
  11a; S. C. 69
 dictionary catalog. S. C. 64
 indention, 8b; S. C. 1-4, 15, 56
 initial capitals, 50b
 main entry under; for anonymous
  books, 2c; S. C. 15
 for anonymous classics, 2m, S.C 16
 for Bible, 11c, S. C. 72
 for cyclopedias, directories and
  almanacs, 2k, S. C. 40
 for periodicals, 2j, S. C. 47
 for sacred books, 2m
 for series, 2n, S. C 31
 numbers in, 4f, S. C. 15, 11, 56, 63
 omissions from, 2e, 4a, 50b, S C 55

partial; added entry for, 2k; S. C 29
punctuation, 51b
rare books, 4g
of series; reference from, 2u; S. C.
 37
  checks for reference, S. C. 36
  on shelf list, 41l, 42c; S. C. A-E,
   sheets *facing* p. 66-67
 spacing, 8l
 spelling, 4e; S. C. 36, 38, 44
 on subject cards, 4a
 translator's name in, 4b
Title entry
 arrangement of cards, 9c
 definition, p 11 [a]
 See also Title ; Title , added entry under ;
   Title, main entry under.
Title marks
 arbitrary, 37
 arrangement of titles, 33a
 definition, p. 11 [a]
 titles with same initial, 33b
 titles beginning with same two letters, 33c
Title-page
 checks, 1a, 2c
 illustrated, 4a
 independent, 5k; S. C. 44-45
Title reference, 2s; S. C. 14
Titles
 hereditary; language of, 3a
  noblemen enterd under, 20
 of honor; abbreviations, 52h
  distinguishing, 3f
  omit from title-page, 4a
  reference from, 20
  official, capitalization, 50h
  personal, capitalization, 52h
Transactions, 2j
Translations, 2g
 arrangement in catalog, 9i

Translator
 added entry under; 2g. 2r; S. C. 6
 check, 1c; S. C. 5
 form of name, 3c
 indention, 8e
 for sacred books, 2m
 arrangement of cards, 11l
 main entry under, 2a
  for Bible, 11c
 name in title, 4b; S. C. 5, 58
 See also Joint editors, commentators,
  translators.
Umlaut
 arrangement in catalog, 9b
 in heading, 9b
 reference for, S. C. 9
 in title, 4e
Vedas, treatment, 2m
Verso, definition, p. 11 [a]
Volume numbers
 on accession book, 22r-s
 for index, 41p
 of series, 2u; S. C. 38
 shelf list, 41g, 41p; S. C. B., sheets
  facing p. 66-67
Volumes
 on added entry cards, 5b; S. C. 6
 in call number, 8m, 31a; S. C. 46, 49
 contents, S. C. 5
 of continuations, 5e; S. C. 47
 missing from set, 5d; S. C. 53
 record on cards, 5a; S. C. 40
 two volumes in one, S. C. 3
 of varying size, 5f; S. C. 50

Waterman's ideal fountain pen, 61c
Withdrawals, noted on accession book,
 22u
Works, arrangement in catalog, 9f

Yellow cards, for criticism, 12

www.ingramcontent.com/pod-product-compliance
Lightning Source LLC
Chambersburg PA
CBHW030907170426
43193CB00009BA/767